BULLETPROOF YOUR EXIT

BULLETPROOF
— YOUR —
EXIT

HOW TO PREPARE YOUR BUSINESS AND YOUR FAMILY FOR A SUCCESSFUL BUSINESS EXIT

RANDY M. LONG, JD, CFP®, CEXP™

ISBN: 978-1-947939-78-3
Printed in the United States of America

Published by Author Source
Kansas City, MO
www.AuthorSourced.com

Praise for Bulletproof Your Exit

"You must read this …MUST!

"If you own a business, or have a *desire* to exit it one day—your first move, before any and all others, should be to get a copy of Randy Long's book: *"Bulletproof Your Exit …How to prepare your business and your family for a successful business exit."* It's an enlightening, exciting (yes, exciting) and interesting read about the steps to take to plan your entire business life. It—planning—is often the step forgotten, as building a business overtakes your work life.

"And it is the step I wish I had taken before starting my foray in the business world. If you are that indefatigable and undeterred person who owns a business, you need a copy of Long's book.

"It is vitally important that people plan their business life every step of the way, and Long sets out a prescription for success that will replace the bitter pills of doing it by the seat of your pants.

"If you have a business exit on the horizon, I strongly recommend you read this short and powerful book to mitigate the risks or circumstances that prevent a successful exit.

"Randy is an amazingly well-studied and thoughtful author, who uses historical illustrations to prove why practicing what he preaches makes enormously good and foolproof sense. As he puts it: "The Golden Rule is golden for a reason. It is the foundation of servant leadership, which is the key hallmark of those who create businesses that last for generations."

"And Randy's points, incredibly and soundly illustrated, are absolutely golden …a must read for planning an exit from your company or contemplating buying another one."

~ **Gary W. Evans,**
Operating Partner, ZRF Partners,
Former President and CEO,
Hiawatha Broadband Communications, Winona, Minnesota

"Randy is a gifted writer with a unique style of illustrating his points via historical stories and current personal experiences, all very entertaining. I co-owned a business for 15 years that had revenues in the $40-$45 million. I wish I would have had Randy's book as a reference and guide long before we sold.

"Every business owner should absolutely read this book and take advantage of the excellent and methodical planning to successfully exit your business. Following Randy's bulletproof plan will give you the opportunity to achieve all your goals, from personal freedom and having peace in your family, to financial independence and leaving a legacy. A definite MUST READ for all entrepreneurs!"

~ **Chuck Salter,**
VP Sales-Marketing
Allegiance Chemicals

"I thought the book was going to be about selling your company but it's really about organizing and adding value to your company so that when you're ready to sell it's worth more. I love the checklists provided on how to make your business and personal life more bulletproof! I realized I need to begin 3 to 10 years out before I was actually ready to sell, and I am excited that I've read this book now, rather than waiting 5 or 10 years when I am ready to retire. I highly recommend this book to all entrepreneurs and business people!"

~ **Dominic Joseph Ahearn,**
Ahearn Signs, Owner

"I wish my father had read this book while he was alive; my life would have been so much better after inheriting the family business! As a banker and entrepreneur, I have spent over 25 years advising business owners and running my own companies. This is a book that will be used time and time again as I continue guiding business owners. Having had exposure to Randy and his amazing process, I can now exhale, knowing my family is in good hands. Not only does Randy prepare the reader with a simple step-by-step process to "sell to the buyer they want, at the time you want, for the price you want;" he provides the reader a step-by-step process of how to add value to the business, prepare the business for the unexpected, and plan wisely and methodically for a successful retirement. Whether you plan to keep your business for life, have your family take over the business, or sell it, this is the book for you. I highly recommend as a must read for every entrepreneur!"

~ Dr. Betty™ Uribe,
Managing Director, JPMorgan Chase; International Best-Selling Author: #Values: The Secret to Top-Level Performance in Business and Life; Entrepreneur; Speaker; FORBES Financial Council

TABLE OF CONTENTS

Author's Note

The single biggest danger facing family businesses is their inability to successfully transfer the wealth of a business to the next generation. In fact, the landscape of history is littered with family businesses whose owners were unable to handle their roles as owners *and* family members. Almost every culture has a saying that communicates this truth. The English version is "shirt-sleeves to shirt-sleeves in three generations." In China, this phenomenon is known as "rice paddy to rice paddy in three generations." My favorite rendition is the Arabic understanding of this phenomenon, which is both poetic and prophetic:

> *The first generation retains the desert qualities, desert toughness, and desert savagery . . . they are brave and rapacious, greatly feared. Under the influence of royal authority and a life of ease, the second generation changes from the desert attitude to a sedentary culture, from privation to luxury and plenty, from a state in which everybody shared in the glory to one in which one man claims all the glory . . . But many of the old virtues remain . . . because they had direct personal contact with the first generation . . . The third generation, then, has (completely) forgotten the period of desert life and toughness . . . Luxury reaches its peak among them . . . In the course of these three generations, the dynasty wears away.[1]*

---

1   Ibn-Ḫaldūn, ʻAbd-ar-Raḥmān Ibn-Muḥammad. "Chapter 3." The Muqaddimah. Princeton, NJ: Princeton U, 1967. N. pag. Print.

The first generation works extremely hard to create and build the family business. The second generation also values hard work, and grows the business and the family assets. But the third generation often squanders the wealth and destroys the business. The numbers are telling: only three percent of family businesses last more than two generations.[2]

This book is not a textbook or a technical guide. Rather, *Bulletproof Your Exit* is a roadmap for owners with businesses worth $5-$50 million, who want to create and leave a legacy that provides for their families and best transitions their businesses, so they can have the freedom and peace of mind to enjoy the rest of their lives. I call those owners BraveHearts, because it takes a leader with a brave heart to pull it off, one who is willing to make the hard choices in business and in life.

The Origin of "BraveHeart"

The term "BraveHeart" holds great significance to me.

I love America and truly believe the founding fathers were BraveHearts; they built our country on the bedrock of independence, faith, and freedom. The early settlers came seeking freedom of religion, freedom from tyranny, and the opportunity for financial independence. Many of America's first families used their newfound freedom to great advantage by creating hundreds of thousands of small businesses, which grew our country into the greatest power the world has ever known. Nowhere else in the world could the average person become their own master through creativity, ingenuity, and hard work. They called it the American Dream.

That dream originated from people who lived under religious and political oppression, the original BraveHearts. I am Scotts/Irish and

---

2   Zellweger, Nason, Nordqvist. From Longevity of Firms to Transgenerational Entrepreneurship of Families: Introducing Family Entrepreneurial Orientation. Retrieved November 2012: (http://c.ymcdn.com/sites/www.ffi.org/resource/resmgr/docs/goodman_study.pdf.)

English, and my cultural history is filled with stories of independence and strength. Even the Roman Empire couldn't conquer my ancestors! One of my favorite historical stories is the Scottish fight for independence, because many of the same character traits are necessary for building a *Bulletproof Exit.*

Around AD 100, The Roman Empire decided it was time to conquer the wild lands of Scotland. The Ninth Legion, 6000 soldiers strong, was sent to do the job. Much to Rome's chagrin, the entire legion disappeared, completely succumbing to the guerilla tactics of the wild Celtic warriors. Unable to advance further, the Romans built Hadrian's Wall as a barrier between themselves and their unconquerable foe.

That spirit lived on in 1297, when William Wallace, the original BraveHeart, defeated a vastly larger army of English noblemen at The Battle of Stirling Bridge. James Webb, the chronicler of the Scottish-Irish legacy, writes of Wallace's brave-hearted character: "Here was a leader who fought not for fame or reward, but in pursuit of his nation's honor."

Wallace exemplified leadership in a way unmatched by the Scottish Lords, who were richer, better-educated, and in superior positions of leadership. He led, not by lording over his followers, but by laying down his life to serve his country. He truly was a BraveHeart! His loyalty and fighting spirit are inspirational, not only for military commanders, but for business leaders, and leaders of all organizations.

My Story

Wallace's legacy, and those of his freedom fighters, is part of my family history. My ancestors were some of the first pioneers to settle southeastern North Carolina. The men and women in my family were strong and tough. The men were brawlers—fiercely independent and self-employed—or pastors bravely leading and guiding their congregations. The women were also brave and strong, and had an unquenchable pioneering spirit. It was into this confusing mix of independence, faith, and fists that I was born.

Small business has always been in my blood, and I've loved it since I was a little boy. Growing up, I learned a great deal by working for small business owners and always aspired to be one. I had a few business ventures of my own in high school and college, like mowing grass, cleaning, and painting houses. One brilliant business venture of mine was selling two-day-old bakery goods to the other athletes in their dorms at night. I was doing quite well until I was shut down by regulations. Apparently, the college did not want competition on campus for their vending machines!

In college, I majored in business, with an emphasis on personal finance. Growing up poor, I was intrigued by the personal finance industry and knew I wanted to learn more about making money and developing strategies to keep it. I was also determined to start a business of my own.

However, I needed some skills first. After graduating, I put on my one and only suit and went down to the office of a Wall Street brokerage firm in Newport Beach, CA. I asked to meet with the branch manager and explained to him the work I wanted to do. The entire time I was talking, he kept looking at a paper on his desk! I thought he wasn't listening to a word I said.

Thankfully, I was desperate and pressed on. After fifteen minutes he stopped me and said, "The main office in New York called me two weeks ago and demanded I fill a position exactly like you just described." He ran his hand through his hair. "It's incredible! I didn't know how I was ever going to find someone in time." He then reached across the desk and handed me the piece of paper. "I guess this is meant for you. The job is yours if you can be in New York in 2 weeks."

After a few years of experience and earning my CFP® (Certified Financial Planner), I sensed a disconnection between what clients needed and how the professional world gave advice. Instead of coordinating and collaborating for the benefit of the client, many professionals worked alone, and failed to consult with other family business professionals. I knew there had to be a better way, so I went to law school to learn more. After graduating from San Joaquin College of Law in 1989, I opened up my own practice and grew in competence as my clients grew in complexity.

For many years I ran two separate businesses in California, located side by side: a legal practice that focused on estate planning and business law, and a wealth management firm that focused on building and preserving family legacies.

In 2007, I moved my wife and five kids to North Carolina to be with my extended family. Several years later, I added the Certified Exit Planning (CExP) designation to my credentials and we opened Long Business Advisors, LLC, in Wilmington, NC. I have the privilege of working with and teaching my children the practice of wealth management, business consulting, and what we call The Bulletproof Exit Process: building a bulletproof business and leaving a successful legacy family.

For over 35 years, I have represented, counseled, and advised hundreds of family business owners to plan for the transition of their companies to the next generation, or to prepare their companies for sale. I believe there will be more demand for The Bulletproof Exit Process than there are qualified advisors.

What You Will Learn From This Book

Bulletproof Your Exit will show you how to plan for the successful transition of your business to your family, or to sell to the buyer you want, at the time you want, for the price you want. Since you cannot choose how long you will live or whether you will stay healthy, your business needs to be bulletproof.

This book presents strategies and tactics that will help you develop your business for peak performance, enabling you to *Bulletproof Your Exit*.

I have also woven my deep love for history into these pages, for illustrations at the opening of each chapter. These stories illustrate that success on the battlefield is all about planning, logistics, and execution; the same is true for building a bulletproof business.

I love working with family businesses. They are the bedrock of our economy, and are under attack today. They are challenged by consolidation, burdened with over-regulation, squeezed by taxation, and assaulted from within by the breakdown of family relationships. As a result, for the first time in 35 years, more businesses are dying than are being created.[3] However, the greatest danger to a family business comes not from without, but from within.

In order to *Bulletproof Your Exit*, families have to work *together* and plan carefully. However, the natural tendency is to maintain the status quo. The problem? Left unattended, relationships break down, quality in business drops, laziness sets in, and money is squandered. If the business is to survive and thrive, family relationships and business solutions must support each other. The truth is, it doesn't matter what generation you represent, you can be the leader your family needs by bulletproofing your family business and its exit strategy!

Will you take on the challenge to lead your family and build a bulletproof business? Do you love your family and business enough to invest in a plan that provides a successful exit? Will you purpose to have the foresight and a willingness to execute that plan? Ultimately, you need to be the kind of person who leaves a legacy your family can be proud of. It takes a BraveHeart to do this … and I challenge you to be that person.

All the Best!

Randy M. Long

---

3   Clifton, Jim. "American Entrepreneurship: Dead or Alive?" American Entrepreneurship: Dead or Alive? Gallup, 13 Jan. 2015. Web. 05 May 2015. <http://www.gallup.com/businessjournal/180431/american-entrepreneurship-dead-alive.aspx>.

CHAPTER 1

Setting Up for Success

Four years after the death of Muhammad in 632 A.D., the second caliph, Omar bin al-Khattab, led the newly united Arab tribes against the Eastern Roman Empire in the world's first Jihad. Thousands of Arabs flooded into Christian Syria, slaughtering and pillaging. Emperor Heraclius quickly raised a large multiethnic army of 30,000 Christian fighters and marched them to Syria. They met 24,000 Muslim forces commanded by Khalid bin al-Walid at the banks of the Yarmuk River in Syria.

Before the battle, Heraclius's general, Vahan, and Khalid met to negotiate. The Romans offered to provide the Arabs with money and food on the condition they leave Syria. "It was not hunger that brought us here," Khalid responded coolly, "but we Arabs are in the habit of drinking blood, and we are told the blood of the Romans is the sweetest of its kind." Needless to say, negotiations broke down and the battle began soon after, lasting six days.

On the final day of battle, Khalid spearheaded a massive Arab cavalry offensive against the heavy infantry on the left flank of the Roman formation. Calamitously, a dust storm blew up during the maneuver. The Arabs, accustomed to fighting in such conditions, used the storm-caused havoc to encircle the Romans. Harried by the enemy cavalry and blinded by the sandstorm, the Roman infantry were quickly trapped.

Realizing they were isolated, the Christian infantry maintained formation and withdrew westward. A crescent of Arabs closed in; behind them, precipitous ravines stopped their retreat. The beleaguered infantry fought valiantly throughout the day, but their hope waned as darkness descended. Relying on night vision honed by years of desert warfare, the Arab cavalry charged at dusk. Ultimately pushed to the edge of the ravine, rank after rank of Roman soldiers fell to their deaths. "The Byzantine army, which Heraclius had spent a year of immense exertion to collect, had entirely ceased to exist," writes British lieutenant-general and historian John Bagot Glubb. "There was no withdrawal, no rearguard action, no nucleus of survivors. There was nothing left."

Following this decisive Muslim victory, the Arabs gobbled up 4000 miles of undefended Roman territory. Indeed, mere decades after Yarmuk, all ancient Christian lands between Greater Syria to the east and Morocco to the west had been conquered by Islam.

* * * * *

Heraclius had no backup plan, no troops in reserve, and no contingency force, leading to his army's obliteration. The Muslims swallowed up a large portion of his empire *because he had never stopped to consider what would happen if he lost Yarmuk.*

While it may seem ridiculous that the leader of the entire Roman Empire would neglect to plan for disaster, it is just as common among business owners. I've seen many businesses wiped out by a failure to prepare for bad-case scenarios, and in doing so, lose their business legacy.

Creating a thriving business legacy is the primary objective of *Bulletproof Your Exit*, and is accomplished through the Bulletproof Exit Process. Successful legacies are founded upon the values and ideals of the business's founder, and are internalized and implemented by the succeeding generation year after year, with structures in place to keep the legacy strong and protected.

Planning for a profitable legacy can be a complicated process, but with the right team of advisors in place, acting in the owner's best interests, the solution is well within reach. The key is to take one step at a time. Our process simplifies the complex, giving the owner the power to take control of when, where, and how to transfer or sell their business through our 7-step process.

The Bulletproof Exit Process

1. Make The Decision – Who, what, why, when, and how much?

2. Assess The Resources – What do you have right now?

3. Assemble The Team – What professionals are you going to use?

4. Create Value Catalysts – How are you going to make your business worth exponentially more?

5. Increase Business Durability – How can you build a *Bulletproof Business*?

6. Live Your Legacy – How will your family benefit from your business?

7. Thrive After Transition – What are you going to do after your business life is over?

The Business Enterprise Institute, located in Denver, Colorado, provides a short quiz to help you assess where you are in the planning process.

1. Do you know how you want to leave the business? Departure date? Desired price? Designated successor?

2. Do you know your income needed to achieve financial security?

3. Do you know how much your business is worth?

4. Do you know how to increase the value of your ownership interest through enhancing the most valuable asset of the company: your employees?

5. Do you know the best way to sell your business to a third party, in order to maximize your cash, minimize your tax liability, and reduce your risk?

6. Do you know how to transfer your business to family members, co-owners, or employees while paying the least possible taxes and enjoying maximum financial security?

7. Have you implemented all necessary steps to ensure that the business continues if you don't?

8. Have you provided for your family's security and continuity if you die or become incapacitated?

If you feel overwhelmed, take heart! Every business owner I have worked with has only been able to answer yes to a few of these questions. However, the continuity of your business and the security of your family depend on you being able to answer yes to each and every one of these questions – and I am here to help you do just that!

If you think you'll have time to figure out your business transition later, think again. For example, a client of mine, Robert Johnson, thought he had all the time in the world to do this, but he never took the time to answer the above questions and it cost him everything.

Robert owned a very successful architectural firm in Florida. He was a devoted husband and a father to a beautiful family. After working hard for many years, he was finally reaping the rewards of his labor. But on April 13th, 2004, tragedy struck. At approximately 8:30 a.m., on his way to visit a client, the firm's private plane went down. At 51 years old, he breathed his last that crisp spring morning—and the future of his business and family changed forever.

Robert loved his work, and sincerely thought he would still be doing the same thing for the next twenty years. He hadn't even considered leaving his business, much less building a *Bulletproof Business* that could withstand tragedy. As a result, his family was devastated, both personally and professionally.

Robert alone held the architectural license for the firm in the tri-state region where his business operated. His skilled employees fled at his death, knowing the firm would not likely survive. His wife was reduced to selling off the physical assets, of which there were few. I promise you, this wasn't the scenario Robert had envisioned when he thought about ending his career. His family mourned the loss of his life and saw the company he loved disintegrate before their eyes, with little to show for his efforts.

As I often tell my clients, "Failing to plan is planning to fail."

The tragic loss of Robert's business could have been avoided. When I asked him to start his exit planning years before, he shook his head and said, "I'm just not ready right now. The business is growing and I already have my hands full with the day to day." I'll never forget him sitting in my office, shaking his head, and telling me he'd get to it later. "I promise I'll start once I have more time," he told me.

"Too busy" might have been his excuse, but it wasn't the real reason. His real problem was that he did not have a strong enough *Why*. You see, Robert never understood why he needed to start planning for the eventual transition of his business. He always thought he had more time. He never understood that the ultimate goal was to make sure his business was bulletproof and that his family could thrive through any crisis.

As unfortunate as it is, stories like Robert's are all too common. Well-meaning, successful business people are forced out of their businesses every day by events beyond their control.

A study by PricewaterhouseCoopers of business owners found that the average owner had 75 percent of their net worth tied up in the business.[4] Despite this huge risk, the survey found that 85 percent of business owners have no exit strategy and 65 percent had no idea what their business was worth.

In fact, according to a 2018 study by the Social Security Administration, a male born in 1966 had a 32 percent chance of becoming disabled

---

4   Mass Mutual Family Business Survey

before reaching retirement and a 9.5 percent chance of dying before reaching retirement age.[5]

What does that mean? Most business owners are just playing the odds. They're betting that they are in the 58.3 percent that make it to retirement without mishap.[6] They are gambling that life will stay the same, and they'll have the time they need to "fix" whatever is broken in their business before they sell or retire, or the economy changes. But life doesn't always work that way – in fact, it rarely does. If you don't have a plan, it's likely you'll get burned.

On an emotional level, I understand why so few owners plan for the worst. It's hard to face the end of your hopes, dreams, ambitions, relationships, and even your own mortality and physical fragility. It hurts to spend money, devote time to the process, and put the work in. At the end of the day, building a *Bulletproof Exit* is a daunting proposition, but it is well worth the sacrifice. Taking time to plan allows you to position yourself to take advantage of life's great opportunities and to be protected from life's great tragedies! When life changes, you'll be ready.

What about you? Do you plan to exit your business in the next three to ten years? What is your exit strategy? Maybe you haven't thought about it that much. Perhaps you have other dreams, but you can't chase them because your business is all consuming. Maybe you are burned out, but you are too young to retire so you just keep grinding away. Or maybe you want to exit this business because you are excited about starting a new one!

Whatever your reason, planning will make that transition easier and more profitable. It will also help you achieve your goals, regardless

---

5   Johanna Maleh, FSA, and Tiffany Bosley, "Table A," *Disability And Death Probability Tables For Insured Workers Born In 1998*, number 2018.6, *August 2018*, https://www.ssa.gov/oact/NOTES/ran6/an2018-6.pdf

6   Johanna Maleh, FSA, and Tiffany Bosley, "Table A," *Disability And Death Probability Tables For Insured Workers Born In 1998*, number 2018.6, August 2018, https://www.ssa.gov/oact/NOTES/ran6/an2018-6.pdf

of what they are. Once you understand why this type of planning is so important, it becomes much simpler to execute. For most of our clients, the "Why" behind it is threefold. It's about (1) Freedom (2) Family and (3) Legacy.

1. Freedom

Most Family business owners agree on one thing: freedom. It is the #1 reason they became entrepreneurs. We interviewed almost a hundred owners in order to write this book, and every single one told us the best thing about owning a business was the freedom, independence, and flexibility it provided.

The sad irony is that many business owners have less freedom than their employees! Instead of owning the business, the business owns them.

You became an entrepreneur because you wanted freedom, opportunity, and time. But even though you make good money, you have less time and less freedom than when you worked for someone else! We built the Bulletproof Exit Process to give you the freedom that you've always wanted. We believe owners should work *on* the business, not *in* it. When you work on the business, you're the master of your own time; which allows you the freedom to take those opportunities, to continue learning, networking, strategizing, creating, discovering and traveling, instead of spending your time grinding away at your desk.

Our goal is to get you out of the day-to-day weeds of the business, help you maximize its value, build it to be bulletproof, and enjoy a lucrative exit.

One of the most underappreciated benefits to engaging in the Bulletproof Exit Process is that it makes your company better, right now, not just when you transition out of it. By the end of the process, you will have:

- Increased the value of your company
- Created retirement and asset management strategies

- Made sure your business and your family are bulletproof
- Strengthened your marriage, and your family bonds

Several years ago, I had the pleasure of working through this process with a client named Tom. Tom's dad had started a successful manufacturing company just before World War II. When his dad died in 1965, Tom took over. One day I approached him and asked, "What are you going to do with the business? Are you ready to sell it?"

Tom replied, "Actually I have been thinking about it for several years because none of my kids want to take over."

Yet despite years of ruminating on it, Tom had never gotten around to actually creating a plan for his eventual sale.

We sat down, talked about his family and business goals, and created a plan to sell the company. We pulled a team of professionals together and we began working to implement the plan. We brought in a CEO to run the business and added "stay bonuses" for a few key employees to ensure they would stay for a year after the sale. Tom spent the final year working *on* the business instead of *in* it. He loved that last year. In fact, his only regret was that he didn't start the process earlier!

We also created a plan for the family that included how Tom wanted the funds distributed after the sale of his company. Tom had plans for what he wanted to do for the years following his retirement, including working on his ranch, traveling with his wife, and spending lots of time with his grandkids. He also wanted to eliminate estate taxes.

We managed to meet all of his objectives because he decided to take action. On the day of his exit, Tom sold his company for the amount he wanted, to the buyer he chose, and within his desired timeframe. This exit provided him freedom to live the rest of his life as he had dreamed— all because he decided to be a BraveHeart and create a *Bulletproof Exit*.

Whether your Bulletproof Business is worth $5 million or $50 million, Tom's story could be yours! With good counsel and smart application of our process, you should be able to transfer your business to the successor you choose, on the date you want, and for the amount you need to comfortably fund your lifestyle.

Ultimately, we want you to run the business so that it's always ready for sale or transition. Once it's ready, it will be worth more, it will run more efficiently, and you will actually be able to enjoy all the benefits of ownership.

2. Family

The second reason owners engage in the Bulletproof Exit Process is to take care of their families. I'm sure you love your family and hope to leave a lasting legacy. But you must plan for it! Planning ahead is worth the effort because it is often the difference between success and failure. Too many business owners forget their family's wealth is tied to the success of the business. They get lost in the weeds, trying to figure out *how* everything will turn out instead of remembering *who* it is all for!

When business owners don't plan well in their business life, the family always suffers. That is why I created the *Bulletproof Exit* Process to operate at the intersection of business and family, *so you can live your legacy today, tomorrow, and for the rest of your life.*

A crucial part of your legacy is the hand off of your business, whether that's a transition to your kids, your employees, or selling to an outside buyer. If you wait until the time is convenient, you'll miss the opportunity to plan for your family's financial future.

Years ago, I met a man who decided to wait. He owned a recreation vehicle dealership, was in his late 30s, married with two kids, and had all the appearance of success. We talked about how to build a saleable business and discussed the need for some planning to ensure the business would be bulletproof, even if he wasn't around. He agreed, walked out of my office, and I never heard from him again.

Eighteen years later, his widow came to my office and told me the tragic news: he had died, the dealership was failing, and she was running out of money. After all that success, he had left her destitute. I don't know what was going through his mind the day we talked; maybe he was too independent, too proud, or just believed nothing could go wrong. No matter his reasons, his wife was the one who would pay for his mistakes.

After looking over her finances, I realized she was going to have to go back to work. I took her by the hand, and told her the truth: There wasn't enough money for their family to live on. Tears rolled down her cheeks as the realization of what she had to do hit her. Her husband had been too independent to take advice and too proud to plan for things out of his control, so she was going to have to pick up the pieces. That sweet lady went back to school, refreshed her skills as a nurse, and provided for her family. She later told me that the stress and fear of going back to work at 55 years old made her cry every single morning for two whole years.

Thankfully, she landed on her feet, and I'm still truly inspired by what she has accomplished. But the truth is, she's never lived in the same luxury she had been accustomed to while her husband was alive. Because of his short-sightedness, she was left unprotected and uncared for after his death. When people ask me why I am so passionate about this process, I remember that wonderful woman and the sacrifices she made to hold her family together.

My hope is that you don't make the same mistake. One day you will exit your business—planned or unplanned! Your exit may come sooner than you expect, whether tragedy strikes or other factors come into play. Regardless, the people most hurt by your procrastination will be your spouse and your kids. So be a BraveHeart and get moving!

3. Legacy

Finally, BraveHeart business owners decide to take on The Bulletproof Exit Process because they want to make a lasting difference in their communities and the world at large. Making charitable donations during the life of the business is one thing, but substantially giving back with the sum of the business sale proceeds or buying a life insurance policy that will benefit your church or favorite charity is something different altogether.

It takes a plan to contribute in a way that lasts beyond your time on earth. How will you use your time, energy, talents, and money in a way that is leveraged across time and space?

While the business may be your main focus today, it's helpful to think about the impact you would like to leave tomorrow. What actions can you take that will make the future a better place for your children and grandchildren?

If you've learned anything from this book so far, it's that failing to plan is planning to fail! You must start now. If you truly desire to leave a legacy, to provide for your family, and to enjoy the freedoms that ownership provides, you have no time to waste! Avoiding to plan is inviting failure or disaster. Over the next ten years, hundreds of thousands of businesses owners will decide to sell or transition … after it's too late.

But it doesn't have to be this way. If you bulletproof your business and provide for a *Bulletproof Exit*, you can provide your family the chance to make the most of the business assets and preserve a lasting foundation that reflects your family ideals and goals. Don't fear your business exit; instead, see it as an opportunity to lay a foundation for a lasting legacy!

Action Steps

- Ask yourself, "Do I want to Bulletproof my business and create a *Bulletproof Exit* that provides for my family and leaves the legacy that reflects who I am?"

If so...

- Review the Bulletproof Exit Process and the questions located on pages 8-9. Answer those you can and determine to get the help you need to answer those you cannot.

CHAPTER 2

STEP 1: Make The Decision

Philadelphia—July 4th, 1776

Fifty-six men sat around a long table, sweat dripping off their powdered wigs in the baking July heat. A sacred hush enveloped the room as the men pondered the impact of their decision. The time had come: Their lives, their fortunes, and their sacred honor were at stake. Something had to be done.

The events leading up to the signing of the Declaration of Independence had precipitated a necessary response. The Boston Massacre was still fresh on the newly born nation's mind. The British had marched in. The midnight ride of Paul Revere had barely saved the budding army from utter annihilation. The clash at Lexington and Concord became the "shot heard 'round the world." And George Washington had stepped up to take the helm as Commander-in-Chief of the Continental Army a mere two months before. Up until now, however, it was merely the uprising of rebel colonies. The Declaration would change everything.

The men huddled around the table knew the effect this document could have. Britain's wrath would soon be unleashed, and full-scale war would quickly be upon them. Signing it would change all their lives. Nine signers would pay the ultimate sacrifice for their names quilled on that brown parchment paper. Seventeen would lose their lands and every last penny.

But one man did not hesitate. With large, swooping swirls, John Hancock inscribed his name on a document that would turn the world upside down. With fire in his eyes, he boldly declared, "There! King George can read that without spectacles; let the British ministry double their reward."

* * * * *

John Hancock knew exactly what he was getting into. He knew the danger, he knew the risk, but he pressed on because he believed the reward was worth it: a nation's freedom for the price of his life. The rest is history!

Business owners face a similar decision about the continuity of their business. Is it worth the time and effort spent planning to build a *Bulletproof Business* and a *Bulletproof Exit*? The stakes may not be life and death, but they are still high. It takes a true BraveHeart to realize the implications, commit to the process, and see it through to the end.

The first step in the Bulletproof Exit Process is to make a decision about the end goal. What do you ultimately desire for your business? What's the end goal? In order to make that decision, *begin with the end in mind and draw your finish line.* Here are three questions to help you:

- When do I want to transition out of my business?
- To whom do I want to sell or leave my business?
- How much money will I need to secure my financial independence?

Creating the finish line may seem like a strange place to start, but it is the most crucial part of the whole process. Yogi Berra once quipped, "If you don't know where you are going, you may not get there." You have to define what a *Bulletproof Exit* will look like for you ... and no one else can do that for you.

> ❝ **It's easier to live in the present and pretend like the future will never come, but the truth is, you will have to exit your business.** ❞

It's easier to live in the present and pretend like the future will never come, but the truth is, *you will have to exit your business*. You can do it admirably, selling for maximum price to an outside seller or proudly handing it off to your kids or employees, or you can do it poorly. Why not do it well? The *Bulletproof Exit* allows you to leave your company so you are fully satisfied in retirement, with assets to enjoy, and a successful business that continues your legacy.

As you address what kind of exit you want, you must also consider how your exit will impact (1) your family and (2) your finances.

The Family Decisions

Before asking yourself financial questions such as, What is the potential selling price of your business? ask yourself the family question: "How will this transition affect my family?" The success of your transition and the stability of your family begin with you. You must also consider how your exit will affect your employees and even your community. The impact will be far greater than you imagine!

My client Keith had to learn this lesson the hard way. Over the course of his career, he had built a sprawling franchise business with nearly 100 different locations. He had three sons, but only one son, John, worked with him in the family business. Keith was a strong personality; I remember how obstinate he was about getting his way. He could never sit down and worked into his late 80s, maintaining an iron grip on the business.

When his health started failing, he had to give control up to John. Unfortunately for everyone involved, Keith had never trained John to run the business, and didn't think about how his plan would affect his family.

Despite my repeated warnings, Keith never let me help him plan for his exit. Instead of taking my advice, he used his own lawyers to help him leave the business equally to his three sons. The day he died, his son John effectively began working for his two brothers—two men who had never spent a single day in the business.

Instead of thinking through his family dynamics, Keith created a family time bomb. The business could have transitioned to John at Keith's death, in acknowledgement for investing his life in running the business. The other two sons could've been fairly treated with an inheritance outside the business. Instead, Keith's poor plan created war within the family. Because he refused to think through the ramifications of his "equality" choice, Keith hurt his family *and* his business, two things he never foresaw or intended.

I've seen kids become so frustrated with the lack of transition planning, they finally take the situation into their own hands. While this at least moves the process along, it does so in a way that often alienates the older generation, who think their children are just after their money. Don't let this happen to you! You need to take the time, energy, and effort to make the right decision for you and your family. If you refuse to make decisions, you are only inviting chaos to ensue.

Businesses and families succeed when the owner puts the needs of others ahead of their own. In short, they implement the Golden Rule. You don't engage in The Bulletproof Exit Process just for yourself; you do it for your family, your employees, and for the continuance of your legacy. And you benefit you as well!

My client, Jacob, is a perfect example of what can happen when families put each other first and create a future for their business.

Jacob had started a tire company shortly after the Vietnam War with some money he was left by his grandfather. His son, Phillip, worked for the business on holidays and summer break while he was in high school and college. After college, he decided to gain some outside expertise and worked at another firm for five years. When Phillip came back to work at the family business, his dad put him on a long-term management track that moved him up systematically over the years.

Shortly after I came in, Jacob turned over operational control of the business to Phillip, but he stayed on board as CEO, strategic mentor, and advisor. He also began working more on the business instead of in it. Jacob went through the entire Bulletproof Exit Process to make sure his entire family and his business would be cared for in case of emergency, while also planning to live a long and good life. Today, the business is flourishing under Phillip's management, and Jacob spends 50 percent of his time traveling and spending time with his grandkids, and 50 percent of the time dreaming up new things for the company to accomplish. That's what it looks like to build a *Bulletproof Exit.*

> **Love your family enough to protect their relationships by planning well for your exit.**

Organizations like Jacob's demonstrate that family and business don't have to be at odds. When integrated correctly, they can be used as a lever to boost both to heights unachievable on their own. A transition that is fully thought through by the founder often results in financial prosperity, business sustainability, and a lasting family legacy. On the other hand, a family business transition that is handled badly can result in litigation, business collapse, family feuding, and a complete breakdown in relationships.

Love your family enough to protect their relationships by planning well for your exit. If you want to avoid irreparable damage to your family and legacy, it is vital that you work through the first step of the Bulletproof Exit Process: The Decision.

STEP 1: THE DECISION

In order to make optimum exit decision, start with your dream goals and then prepare in a way that maximizes the end result, both personally and financially.

The Financial Decisions

Once you have settled the family issues, it's time to determine how much money you need to live your ideal lifestyle. A word of warning: Most advisors plan on your expenses declining after retirement. In my experience, most clients maintain their standard of living or increase it, which means most people underestimate the amount of cash they need after exiting their business.

It's easy to forget the little expenses that are tied up in the business. Once you sell, you won't be able to drive the company car or expense your health care. Instead, you'll have to pay for them with your own, after tax dollars. Obviously, your age at exit will drastically change these numbers.

Don't rely on estimated average expenses when determining how much money you will need in retirement. *Average expenses are for average people*, not for business owners. In fact, business owners often spend 25 percent more after they sell their businesses. For instance, consider my client Ryan.

Ryan came to see me some years after selling her business. When I looked at her numbers, it was clear someone had underestimated her expenses after sale, and she was struggling to live out of a portfolio of stocks and bonds. The culprit turned out to be her CPA. The CPA had used generic estimates of what people spend in retirement and underestimated her cost of living by 30 percent! He had also forgotten to factor in all the expenses that Ryan was running through the organization. Once the company was gone, she was left paying for those expenses out of pocket.

The hard reality for business owners is that it takes a different skill set to live out of an investment portfolio than it does to live out of a business's cash flow.

Again, timing is of key importance. When do you want to leave? When will you be financially able to leave? Will you be emotionally ready to leave?

Engaging in the Bulletproof Exit Process is not for the faint of heart, but you don't have to undertake it alone. I work with my clients every step of the way to help them accurately predict the amount they will need to retire comfortably, factoring in inflation, healthcare costs, tax rates, cost of living, expected market returns, goals and expectations, retirement date, and charitable giving.

> **"Engaging in the Bulletproof Exit Process is not for the faint of heart, but you don't have to undertake it alone."**

The Bulletproof Exit Process is all about realism. Instead of guesswork, the process will help you estimate the right time to exit, understand the risk, and err on the side of more cash flow. Engaging in the Bulletproof Exit Process may mean the difference between having a fulfilling retirement with the ability to pursue your own interest, or being forced to return to work for someone else because you ran out of money.

The truth is, you probably need more from a sale than you think. Too many business owners don't understand how much it actually costs them to live. As a result, business owners often sell their company for less than they need to live the lifestyle they desire. Business valuations, personal balance sheets, and cash flow plans are necessary to truly understand where you are, and how much it takes to live the life you dream. Don't be afraid to pause, take a step back, and understand the gap that exists between where you are now and where you want to be. Create a plan to bridge the gap and go after it!

Action Steps

- When do you want to transition out of your business?
- Do you plan to transition to your child, employee or sell to a third-party?
- What does your lifestyle look like once you retire?
- Is your current advisor qualified and experienced in Exit Planning?

CHAPTER 3

STEP 2: Assess Your Resources

Evaluating Business and Personal Wealth

In the spring of 1982, Argentina invaded the Falkland Islands. President Leopoldo Galtieri decided his fellow Argentines needed a little boost to their nationalistic pride, and what better way than to win back long-lost territory? Additionally, economic issues were brewing on the home front and Galtieri thought his country needed a diversion. His plan was simple: invade the islands just off Argentina's coast and take back their "homeland" from the far-off ruling empire of Britain.

Surprisingly, his plan initially worked. The small garrison of Royal Marines was surprised by the chutzpah of the neighboring Argentines and was forced to surrender after two days of fighting. Victory was quick and sweet.

But as with most ill-planned escapades, President Galtieri had grossly underestimated the size and scope of the British retaliation. 127 ships filled with 12,000 men were sent under Margaret Thatcher's orders to reclaim the empire's lost lands. "Black Buck" raids began immediately with RAF Vulcan bombers lighting up nearby airstrips and Argentine ships. Mere days into the conflict, British destroyers had blown up two of Argentina's submarines, forcing the navy to retreat to its South American shores.

9,000 British soldiers landed on the Falkland beaches, fighting their way east until the capital city was surrounded. In one skirmish on

Mt. Kent, 600 British commandos would outfight 1,000 Argentines. Encircled on land and sea, with victory wrenched from his grasp, Gen. Mario Menendez was forced to surrender the 9,800 Argentine men under his command. Three months later, President Galtieri was removed from office. The entire war lasted less than 30 days.

* * * * *

As foolish as it was to attack the British Empire with no provocation and no planning, it is almost as bad to try exiting from your company without proper foresight. The Argentines were outmatched and outgunned, and the conflict was over almost before it begun. If the Argentines would have sat down and taken stock of their resources, they would never have risked so much to gain so little. Counting the cost can make the difference between victory and defeat—in war and in business.

> **Counting the cost can make the difference between victory and defeat—in war and in business.**

This is a great illustration as to why no business owner should ever make large business decisions without forethought. Seems obvious, right? Yet most business owners sell their business without much planning or foresight, even though it is likely *the largest financial decision they will ever make.*

Stop and think about this for a moment. Business owners, on average, have 70-90 percent of their net worth tied up in their business. "Sale day" is their one chance to realize the full value of all of their blood, sweat, and tears. Yet too many have no idea what the business is actually worth when they put it up for sale!

This is exactly why step 2 in our process is to assess your resources—starting with your business.

Do you know how much your business is worth? How do you know? Putting a price tag on your business is much harder than most people think. Valuations are more art than science, and can be quite difficult. This is why I strongly advise you to have an appraisal firm value your business from an unbiased perspective. Do not simply rely on your back of the napkin calculations, best guesses, or "industry standards."

Industry standards never hold up during sale negotiations. I often have clients tell me, "Well, my firm is worth such-and-such because firms sell for five times EBITDA in my industry" (EBITDA: earnings before interest, tax, depreciation and amortization). At best, industry standards are a useful comparison tool. At worst, supposed industry standards are misleading and an obstacle that must be overcome when presenting your firm's unique value to a prospective buyer.

Just remember, no one buys a business based on industry averages. If your company sells, it will be based on the unique circumstances and profit potential of your business and its particular assets.

In my experience, business owners rarely know what their business is worth, mainly because they don't think it's worth the time or the money for a formal appraisal.

However, if you're even *considering* selling your business, running an unbiased appraisal helps you to determine the feasibility of your goals. If you are planning to retire on ten million dollars, but your appraiser thinks your business is worth half that, you clearly have work to do.

> **What would make my business worth enough to meet my financial goals?**

Owners that are looking to sell to an outside party often ask, "What's my business worth?" While this is a fine question, here is a better one to ask: "What would make my business worth enough to meet my financial goals?" Your business is worth whatever someone is willing and able to pay for it. Valuation techniques will help you determine a ballpark estimate for a sale price that will help you to plan and forecast, but it isn't until you receive cash in the bank that you will truly know what the business is worth. Until then, focus on creating as much value as possible in your business *before* your transition.

Despite all the uncertainty surrounding business value, it may be the less problematic of the two sides of a business owner's life. Personal evaluation can be just as difficult or even more so.

Personal Net Worth

Once you've accurately assessed your business assets, it's time to look at the personal side. The rest of your net worth is considered personal assets, both financial and non-financial. Assessing these resources is just as important as valuing the business. If the business went under, what would you have left? In other words, is your family financially bulletproof? Business owners often get so wrapped up in the business transition process, they forget to manage and utilize their personal assets as part of the plan.

It is important for you to understand what you have, how it is held, and why you have it. Having both spouses understand this will increase communication and help you make decisions in the planning process. Too often, I get different answers from spouses about what a certain pool of money is set aside to accomplish. One person may think it's for a down payment on their next house, while the other is reserving it for retirement. Obviously, this can cause a lot of problems in the future. Until you know what the funds are for, you cannot know whether you have enough money to retire successfully.

Several years ago, a friend referred me to a husband and wife who were culturally very different. The wife was Greek and the husband was German. I quickly realized that whenever they discussed money, the wife would become very expressive with both her voice and her body language. The husband, in return, would become rigid, stone-faced, and look away from her, because he could not deal with the drama. I decided to separate them, and discuss one-on-one to see if there was a way for them to work together.

I looked at their assets and noticed a rather large pool of capital that wasn't being put to use, so I asked both to write down how they would use those specific funds. After fifteen minutes, I took both sheets of paper, looked them over, and then gave the two spouses each other's answer sheet. Once they had looked over the sheets, I then had each spouse explain how he or she came up with the list.

This exercise helped them understand that they did not have the money to do everything they both wanted to do. Instead, they would have to make compromises and decisions for the good of the family—together.

Once I helped the husband and wife team to start thinking as a family instead of as two individuals, the conversation reached a turning point. It became about listening and understanding, forgiving and learning to love each other through how they agreed to use family funds, instead of competing for what they each wanted.

"
The most valuable resources you possess are the talents, experience, drive, and abilities of your family members and your health. "

No matter how it feels sometimes, financial resources are never your most valuable personal assets. The most valuable resources you possess are the talents, experience, drive, and abilities of your family members and your health.

Assess Your Human Assets

If you are considering an inside transition, you need to assess the abilities of your successor *before* assuming they have what it takes to run your business. Do they have the talent to grow the company? Do they have the management skill to guide your employees? An accurate assessment of your successor is key; a misunderstanding in this area can sideline the entire process.

In one case I worked on, the successor's talents and abilities weren't in question, but rather his will. Jeremy had come to see me about selling his bottling company to Glen, a key employee, since Jeremy had no children. He was so sure about Glen's abilities that he wasn't interested in having me meet with Glen to discuss the transfer. In fact, we worked on the plan for seven months before I finally met him.

When we finally sat down with him, Glen told me: "I hope you don't think I want this company." We were all shocked! He let me know that his plan was to retire in the next 2-3 years, and work on his side business. He was intrigued to find Jeremy was planning to transition the business to him, *since they had never even had a conversation about it.* Needless to say, Jeremy was not happy. We ended up going back to the drawing board and realigning the process to work toward a sale to a third party. We wasted a lot of time, energy, and money walking down a path that wasn't even available.

The same thing can happen in family transitions. Parents often assume their son or daughter is going to take over the business, but they never sit down to have an exploratory conversation! The need for honesty in this step is paramount. Regardless of your heirs' interest, do they have the capability to run the business? Do they need more schooling or time to learn the ropes? Do they have the desire? Have you fostered an atmosphere where they can tell you what they *really* think instead of what you want to hear? Assessing personal worth and human assets can be the difference between success and failure in the end.

Determining and evaluating the resources you have at your disposal is key to formulating a winning strategy. Without an accurate place to start, you cannot know how to begin, where the finish line is, or even where it should be!

War is all about logistics and preparation; so is The Bulletproof Exit Process. You will miss many opportunities and leave money on the table if you do not prepare in advance.

> **Don't go to war, don't build a tower and don't exit a company without proper plans and preparations.**

The Bible tells us that a foolish man begins to build a tower without understanding how much it will cost. When he runs out of money, the half-built tower witnesses to the world that he did not plan well.

Don't go to war, don't build a tower and don't exit a company without proper plans and preparations.

Before you move on to the next step, take some time to assess your financial resources and your potential successors.

Action Steps

- Hire a professional appraiser to do a formal valuation of your company.
- Create a list of your personal assets and discuss the purpose of each with your spouse and key advisors.

CHAPTER 4

STEP 3: Assemble The Team

Paris, France—April 9th, 1694

Centuries before Bernie Madoff created the largest Ponzi scheme in US history, a renegade Scot fast talked his way into the confidences of the most powerful king in contemporary history—and along the way pulled off the greatest con the world had ever seen. His name was John Law.

Law was the son of a simple banker but preferred more extravagant pursuits over sober-minded finance and the family business. On April 9th, 1694, he killed a man in a duel over a woman and was sentenced to death. He managed to escape, however, and spent the next several years traveling Europe, gambling everywhere he went. He eventually landed in Paris, rubbing shoulders with the French elite. It was in the Parisian dens of the idle rich that he met the most powerful man on the continent: Duke Phillippe d'Orleans.

Law was able to catch the attention of the Duke with his brilliant financial mind and forward-thinking economic theories. In 1720, d'Orleans appointed Law as Controller General of Finances, which gave Law complete mastery of the French national debt, collection of all taxes, the country's 26 coin mints, and most importantly, the Louisiana colony. The fox was now in the hen house.

From this power base, Law created the Mississippi Company, which had exclusive rights to trade with the Louisiana Colony. Law's PR campaign painted Louisiana as a veritable wonderland of riches. The campaign paid off and company shares rocketed to over 60 times their original value, making Law the richest man in France.

Unfortunately, when the settlers recruited by Law arrived in Louisiana, they found only swamps and sickness waiting. Eighty percent of them died of tropical diseases and starvation. Word spread quickly to Paris and the shares of the Mississippi Company plunged. Angry crowds gathered outside of Law's bank, throwing rocks and breaking windows. The situation became so desperate that Law fled the country, leaving the French economy in shambles. The kingdom's finances never recovered. Louis the XV died soon after, leaving his grandson Louis the XVI in command of a bankrupt French Monarchy. Fifteen years later, the French peasantry rose up in one of the bloodiest revolutions in World History. The bloodshed would not stop until the fall of Napoleon in 1815.

* * * * *

When the Duke of Orleans appointed John Law as General Controller of France, he had no idea that his incredibly poor selection of an advisor would pave the way for the downfall of his entire country! In many ways, owning a business is a bit like running a small-scale economy. Having good advisors is as important for a business owner as it is for a monarch.

> **The quality of advisors selected can make or break the exit plan you create for your business.**

In order for your business to thrive, you are going to need a team that has your best interests at heart and is well-suited for your family and company needs. This is extremely important, because the quality of advisors selected can make or break the exit plan you create for your business.

Step 3 of the Bulletproof Exit Process is to assemble your team of professional advisors.

The bigger the business being transitioned, the wider and deeper a team's knowledge and experience needs to be. The stakes are high—the majority of your net worth is at risk. It is imperative that you have high caliber professionals to make sure the transition is a success.

First and foremost, you need a planner with a deep and wide background across a variety of disciplines. Why? You need someone to plan with you who can consider the entire picture. Most practitioners work in one or two areas, but you need someone who has expertise in the fields of finance, tax, insurance, and law. You need someone who can integrate business planning, estate planning, and wealth management so your business and your family are ready for your moment of triumph. Remember, your *Bulletproof Exit* is the single most financially critical point in your career.

Before we get into specific team member roles, it is time to step back and ask yourself: "Why should I use advisors in my business transition?" After all, you are a very successful businessperson who is used to being in charge. You have vast experience brokering deals, buying and selling equipment, moving inventory and much more. You are competent at running your business, so why wouldn't you be qualified to manage a sale or transition? Good advisors do not come cheap; the more qualified and skilled they are, the more money they charge.

> " **The skills needed to run a business are very different from those needed to transition it.** "

While price is an issue, we will address that valid concern last. The problem with running your own transition is that the skills needed to run a business are very different from those needed to transition it. You have done an excellent job working on your business, but if you are like most owners, you have never sold a business, drafted an estate plan, provided key tax advice, or built a *Bulletproof Business* that is always ready for sale.

Simply put, the highest and best use of your time and talents is not in selling a business or planning a transition. Instead, your energy should be devoted to running the business and making sure it's humming along perfectly when you're ready to sell.

As a result, you are going to need the services of experts whose education, training, and experience will help you can make wise decisions and achieve your exit goals.

The best example of the danger of running your own process is from a man named Cameron. Several years ago, Cameron walked into my office and asked if I could manage some money for him. He had just sold his company and wanted to see if we could help transfer money to his kids in a tax efficient manner. Naturally, I was curious to hear the story of the sale, so we sat down and he told me how it all unfolded.

He had two important advisors in his life at the time: a CPA who prepared his taxes for him and a lawyer who had handled some real estate issues for him. Both were his friends, so when he decided to sell the company, he sought their advice.

The problem was, their advice conflicted and he had no help in understanding the discrepancies. Instead of paying for an expert to craft a plan, Cameron decided to merge the two plans together. The lawyer attempted to serve as the deal lawyer and the accountant did his best to minimize taxes. Unfortunately, it was clear from his discussion that neither the CPA nor the lawyer understood much about preparing for a sale or running an auction process.

Cameron's method of trying to take advice from different professionals to create his own plan turned into a mess. The sale was complete, but he ended up with only 50 percent of what his business was most likely worth.

He also missed opportunities to plan for his family and long-term employees. In the end, the buyer and the IRS got a great deal, but Cameron's attempt at saving money in professional fees cost him a lot of money. As the saying goes, "You get what you pay for."

Instead of managing the process yourself, you should first hire a planner to run the process and take their lead in engaging an M&A firm, an estate planning attorney, a business attorney, etc. so you can get the most value from your *Bulletproof Exit Plan.*

The Business Team

It's important to understand the players on your team, and the role they need to play in order for you to ultimately win at the time of transition.

We'll start with the Exit Planner. The Exit Planning Advisor (who we call the Bulletproof Exit Planner) is the one who puts the plan in motion, monitors progress, brings the team together, acts as the owner's primary representative, and facilitates the sale or transition process. The Bulletproof Exit Planner stands by the owner's side at every step of the way to make sure he crosses the finish line a winner.

As such, the Bulletproof Exit Planner's primary role is to coordinate the entire process. If you have chosen to exit via a third-party sale, then the Bulletproof Exit Planner will help you prepare the company for sale, hire the M&A firm, manage your expectations, and walk with you through the entire turbulent process. A third-party sale involves much preparation and hard work, not to mention the emotional roller coaster ride it provides. In most deals, it is common for the deal to die several deaths before the final paperwork is signed. If you are selling to a third party, be prepared for a process that is highly complex and awash in high-pressure decision making.

The goal for the Bulletproof Exit Planner is to bring together an all-star team of advisors. Most owners only get one shot at transitioning, so they need as much talent as possible on their side.

You may be thinking, "If I have all these expert team members, why do I still need a Bulletproof Exit Planner?"

Let's ask this another way: If the athletes are so good, why do they need a coach?

One of my favorite stories is the perfect answer to this question. It's the riveting tale of America's quest for basketball gold in the 1992 Olympics. For the first time ever, the Olympics were allowing professional basketball players into the games, and America was determined to win.

Unfortunately, most of the NBA players didn't want to be in the Olympics, and they most certainly didn't want to play together. They needed someone who could bring them together, who understood their strengths and weaknesses, and could help them get past their petty rivalries to win Olympic gold.

They didn't need better players. They needed a coach. They needed Chuck Daly.

When Chuck took over the USA basketball team in 1992, not one NBA player would join the Olympic team. But after a series of genius maneuvers, Chuck had convinced the greatest superstars to play: Michael Jordan, Scottie Pippen, Magic Johnson, Larry Bird, Patrick Ewing, Charles Barkley, John Stockton, Clyde Drexler, and the infamous Christian Laettner.

Now, you might think his job was over. Why would players like that need a coach? As it turned out, getting them to say yes was only half the battle. NBA rivalries and their superstar egos were getting in the way of them playing like a team. In fact, leading up to the Olympics, they even lost to a college basketball team!

But Chuck wasn't about to let them lose gold. He was creating a team that would become legendary. By the end of the 1992 Olympics, Chuck had brought the greatest team in basketball together, and their run to win Olympic gold would go down in history books as "The Dream Team."

> **You need a good coach, the right people to play on your team, and you need everyone to play their roles in a team-like manner so you can win in the end.**

In much the same way, the Bulletproof Exit Planner's goal is to help you win Olympic gold with your dream team. The truth is, the world of business isn't much different from basketball. You need a good coach, the right people to play on your team, and you need everyone to play their roles in a team-like manner so *you* can win in the end.

A truly competent Bulletproof Exit Planner functions like a general contractor. They assist you in understanding the plans, hiring the roles that need to be filled (plumber, electrician etc.) and overseeing the work so your dream house goes according to plan. The goal is simple: make your dream become a reality.

In addition to the Bulletproof Exit Planner, you will also need two to three lawyers. Whether you like lawyers or not, you need them on your team. They will address two vital areas: the sales transaction and the structure of your estate. For these two functions, you will need at least one M&A lawyer and one estate planning lawyer.

The estate planning lawyer must be one of the first professionals to consider as you begin planning. There are certain strategies and planning opportunities that must be completed for the family estate plan before you even contemplate a sale. This is one of the primary reasons why the Bulletproof Exit Process can take a number of years and should not be rushed, especially for a family whose wealth is in excess of $10 million dollars, or if the family has a fast-growing company.

The next player on your team needs to be a competent accounting firm that can provide strong tax advice. Because of the due diligence that naturally accompanies a sale, the sooner an accounting firm is involved, the better. You will also need a good M&A firm with strong accounting skills to make sure the financials are in shape and ready for the sale. Buyers will want to know every nitty gritty detail of your business, so you can expect a thorough due diligence process that will get into the weeds!

Being prepared for the sales process will not only make life easier for you, but it should also help you get a better price for your company. Issues found in due diligence often reduce the sale price, sometimes even retroactively. Buyers love to use the due diligence process to find "problems" that drive down the purchase price. One of their favorite tricks is to "discover" some issues right around closing when you are already mentally and emotionally committed to a sale, and thus willing to accept a lower price just to get the deal done.

" It's best to know what the buyer will find before they do! "

We prepare our clients for a rigorous due diligence process by a third-party buyer. It's best to know what the buyer will find before they do! Hire an accounting firm and a law firm to go through your documents and look for any issues that may be present. By being proactive, you can identify issues and minimize potential risks that could derail the deal later on. A problem that can be discovered and fixed before the buyer finds out will guarantee a smoother ride.

The Family Team

Just like your business team, you are going to need a team of professionals to help your family plan. At the very least, you must have one in each of the following categories: (1) estate planning lawyer; (2) CPA; (3) personal insurance professional; (4) wealth manager and of course; (5) a Bulletproof Exit Planner.

A top-notch business law and estate planning firm can provide business and tax advice that will save you money in more ways than you can imagine. Don't be dissuaded by the price! I've personally seen these professionals save over $40 million dollars in estate and income taxes for one family. Key point: make sure your professionals are planning with you, not just taking orders or keeping records.

You also need to hire insurance professionals who can identify and structure a plan that leverages the entire range of property, casualty, and life insurance products to protect risks in multiple areas.

A wealth management or a multi-family office will be necessary to provide investment management and other services once the sale is completed. Be sure that your wealth management advisor truly provides full-service management. *Many advisors call themselves wealth managers, but do not have the education or experience to help you at your level of complexity!* The needs of a business owner sometimes outgrow their wealth manager's abilities and advice levels. Just be aware that it could be a problem.

Your wealth manager must be able to help you determine what amount you will need, net of all costs and taxes, in order to live the life you have planned. While this sounds simple, it is much harder than you think. It is so easy to make false assumptions and build a plan around them, yet doing so leads to disaster.

Finally, it is vital that you have a Bulletproof Exit Planner (or other exit planning professional) that understands both the business impact of your exit and the personal impacts as well. Your Bulletproof Exit Planner needs to work with the family and business teams, coordinating the two teams so they are working together.

Your advisors need to possess these two characteristics in order for you to consider them for your all-star team: competence and teamwork mentality. The professionals you work with need to be competent in their respective fields, able to communicate efficiently and effectively with each other, and ultimately, be able to work together.

> **Your advisors need to possess these two characteristics in order for you to consider them for your all-star team: competence and teamwork mentality.**

All of your advisors should expect to be part of a team and not isolate you from the other advisors. That kind of conduct should be a red flag for you. If they do not want to work with other advisors, it may be because they have an agenda, or they are afraid that you may discover that they really don't know what they are doing. Either way, you end up with a mess. The best mix is to find an advisor who is constantly looking out for your well-being, has the expertise to help you make wise decisions for you and your family, and can help you build and manage the professional team you need.

The beauty of The Bulletproof Exit Process is that you have the ability to observe the planning and implementation as the case progresses. Too many plans just get written up and put on a shelf. *With The Bulletproof Exit Process, we make sure we're executing every step of the way.* If you hire a different exit planner, make sure he or she is implementing as you go along, and not just providing a plan that gathers dust.

Finally, it's important to see your family members as team players. Many business transitions have gone awry because a spouse wasn't on board with the process or thought it should be handled another way. A strong spousal relationship can be a key asset for the exit process, giving helpful perspective on major decisions that must be made. On the other hand, a weak spousal relationship can be the death of a hard-negotiated sale.

> **A strong spousal relationship can be a key asset for the exit process, giving helpful perspective on major decisions that must be made.**

I remember a transaction I worked on many years ago with a family that was selling their business to a third party. The husband assured me that his wife did not need to be included in any of our discussions, despite my objections. He stood his ground, completely convinced that all she needed to do was sign her name at the close, so we moved forward in the negotiations without her.

The day of the closing came and my conference room was packed with lawyers. My client sat in front of a long table filled with documents. We had been through an emotional sale process and everything was all settled—until his wife came storming in. She marched right up to the head of the table and declared she wasn't signing anything because not a single person had consulted her during the entire process. The husband's refusal to include his wife put the deal back an entire month, resulted in thousands of dollars of extra legal fees, and almost cost him the sale.

Securing family buy-in early is essential to creating a team-like atmosphere throughout the transition. *Keep the end in mind.* When the process is over, retirement will be much more enjoyable if your spouse has been happy the entire time! Keep your spouse and key family relations not just in-the-know, but also a part of the larger decisions that come your way through the process. Remember, a planned exit should strengthen family ties, not sever them.

Action Steps

- Make a list of family members who will be impacted by your exit strategy.
  - Have you had conversations with each person or held a family meeting?
  - Are you taking into account their thoughts and desires?
  - Note: You may also need to do this step with certain key employees.

- Make a list of your current business and family advisors.
  - Do they have the competence and expertise to pull off a business sale or a transition? Are they willing to be team players to get the job done?

- Make a list of the team members you are missing.
  - Do you have a planner that can help you hire the missing members?

With a strong team of advisors and family members on board, you are well on your way to a successful exit!

CHAPTER 5

STEP 4: Create Value Catalysts

May 16th, 1940

World War One was the war to end all wars. Raging for four and a half brutal years, the Great War devastated Europe. Soldiers on both sides were put through hell—fighting through freezing winters, scorching summers, long nights, empty stomachs, and pain and misery on a scale never seen before. By the end of the war, over 9 million men had been killed, with another 21 million wounded. The country of France was literally decimated, with around 11 percent of its population killed or wounded. The French high command vowed that they would never again face such misery.

To accomplish this, the French established a line of concrete fortifications, obstacles, and weapons installments along the border of Germany, Luxembourg, and Switzerland known as the Maginot Line. The strategy behind the Maginot line was simple: make it impossible to launch an offensive on the French border.

French military experts called the Maginot Line a work of genius. They believed it would allow the French army enough time to mobilize in response to any threat. The Line truly was a feat of engineering. It was impregnable to most forms of attack available at the time, including aerial bombings and tank fire. The fortifications had state-of-the-art living conditions for garrisoned troops, air conditioning, comfortable eating areas, and underground railroads. Yet for all of its wonderful accommodations and impervious defenses, the Maginot Line was a strategic disaster.

The German military generals of WWII knew their business well. Instead of attacking the line directly, the Germans simply went around it. Hitler ordered his Panzer divisions to bulldoze straight through the Ardennes forest and the Low Countries in a move the French thought impossible. German Blitzkrieg tactics caught the French completely off guard, forcing the army to surrender in a matter of weeks. Within a month and a half, the entire country of France was in German hands.

* * * * *

The French believed they were making investments that counted, but in the end, true value would have been found in modern equipment, planes, and armored artillery rather than outdated concrete walls. The Germans invested heavily in modern technology and as a result, smashed through French defenses. The Germans, not the French, built what mattered. The Value Catalysts the French ignored ultimately cost them their freedom.

"Value Catalyst" is a term I've coined to describe structures and strategies that have an exponential impact on organizations. You will hear other speakers and authors talk about value drivers or business drivers, but I find those terms too constraining. Value Catalysts are not limited to business, and they do more than simply add zeros to the end of a sale price. Catalysts in chemical reactions spark change. They jumpstart a chain of events, and the same is true of Value Catalysts. A Value Catalyst is a process or person that creates more energy, time, and money than it takes in. Implementing Value Catalysts can truly change the direction and the quality of your life and help you build a true *Bulletproof Business.*

> " **Self-sustaining, bulletproof businesses sell for much higher multiples than those that rely on the owner.** "

Value Catalysts are the structures, people, and processes that help owners work <u>on</u> their business instead of <u>in</u> it. Effective Value Catalysts are the difference between true owners and glorified managers. Do you have a business that can grow without you? Suppose you left for six months—vacation, sickness, travel, side ventures—would your business survive? If you have any hesitation answering that question, it is unlikely that your business has the Value Catalysts it needs. Keep this in mind: *Self-sustaining, bulletproof businesses sell for much higher multiples than those that rely on the owner.*

Owners in the midst of a transition are not the only ones that benefit from Value Catalysts. All businesses are created to build value for their owners, so all businesses, in any stage, should be working on creating Value Catalysts. In this chapter we will explore the Value Catalysts that make the most difference in both business and family.

Business Value Catalysts

Building Value Catalysts starts long before you intend to exit your business. For this reason, we recommend beginning the Bulletproof Exit Process three to seven years before your planned exit. This may sound shocking to you! But some changes—such as tax strategies—have to be made even ten years before a transition.

Don't tune out just yet. *It is worth the time, energy, and effort it takes to put these things in place years in advance.* Even if you don't have that kind of time, any effort you make into enhancing these Value Catalysts will have a significant return on investment.

The most important business Value Catalysts consist of the following:

- Stable and motivated management team
- Diverse customer base
- Facility appearance
- Financial controls
- Proprietary technology
- Growth in cash flow
- Realistic growth strategy

Buyers seeking to acquire your *Bulletproof Business* will look at these key metrics when determining a value for which they are willing to pay. Businesses without Value Catalysts represent huge risks for acquirers.

Stable and Motivated Management

The single most important Value Catalyst in your business is your management team. It is from this one Catalyst that all others will flow. You need a management team on which you can rely, one that can eventually run the business without you. It takes a team—well-oiled and disciplined—to implement strong Value Catalysts and keep them working consistently to increase the value of your business.

If you have built your entire company around your own skills and expertise, you can make good money, but the company is never going to grow beyond you. You will end up having trouble selling or transitioning for a good price because there will be nothing to actually buy. Once you leave, the business will likely fold.

Take it from Bruce. Bruce ran a large cattle operation in the Central Coast of California and ruled it with an iron fist. Though his son, Art, worked for him, he refused to surrender any control of the company and micromanaged all aspects. Art was a hard worker and a loyal son. But he did not want to confront his dad, so he just became bitter.

43

It was only after Bruce's death at 87 that Art was able to run the cattle operation. By that time, he was 65 years old. The family implications were heart-breaking. Even after his father's death, Art was unable to shake the negative and bitter attitude he'd developed working under Bruce. Instead of a business that built a family legacy rooted in love, Bruce had built a business that tore it apart.

> ## If you refuse to train and delegate, you will build a prison instead of a castle.

Bruce and Art's story constantly reminds me that it is vital to build up your family and your management team with positive encouragement and mentoring. *If you refuse to train and delegate, you will build a prison instead of a castle.*

Diversified Customer Base

A diversified customer base is seen by buyers as adding value and reducing risk. Just like in investing, diversification lowers risk. If you only have a few customers, you are exposing buyers to the very real and high risk that one of those customers will leave with you. Even if a buyer is willing to purchase your business with limited customers, he will probably structure the deal to include significant earn outs or holdbacks to minimize that risk.

Facility Appearance

Your facility appearance should be consistent with your asking price. With this Catalyst, I often have clients scratch their heads. Owners are thrifty people who only spend money when they know it will make them more money. They are often reluctant to spend cash flow on facility appearances, especially if the space is not often visited by the general public. However, businesses (just like houses) need some curb appeal to sell.

The reason I include facility appearance in Value Catalysts is because buyers make decisions based on a combination of emotional and logical reasons. When people are house hunting, things such as a fresh paint job and an uncluttered space can make an outsized impact. The same goes for businesses. A good-looking facility can convey your company culture, extend your brand image, explain your message of excellence, and provide an., opportunity for you to market your company to buyers. If it looks sloppy on the outside, they may assume the inside of the company is run in a sloppy manner as well.

Financial Controls

The existence of reliable financial controls is a Value Catalyst often overlooked. Documented controls not only safeguard the company's assets but are also an invaluable tool for management. Any potential buyer will sift through your financials with a fine-tooth comb. If the buyer is not completely comfortable with the numbers, he will either give you a lowball offer or call the whole thing off. Buyers know that numbers do the real talking. The more confidence they have in your numbers, the more cash they will fork over.

> " **Buyers know that numbers do the real talking.** "

Proprietary Technology

Control of proprietary technology can make the value of a business far greater than the capitalization of historical earnings. Take it from my friend, John Brown, who I consider the father of exit planning. In his book, *Cash Out and Move On,* he tells of one client named Will Rogers who quadrupled the value of his business solely based on the development of proprietary technology.[7]

---

7   Brown, John H., Kevin M. Short, and Kathryn B. Carroll. *"Get Top Dollar—And More—Selling Your Business." Cash out Move On: Get Top Dollar, and More, Selling Your Business.* Golden, CO: Business Enterprise Institute, 2008. 108-09. Print.

According to John, Will owned a small systems engineering firm that designed and installed cellular networks. Like many small service businesses, Will's company had a sporadic earnings history. The most recent three years' profit and cash flow had been declining and Will had been told by his CPA that the business did not have much value.

On the surface, I would have agreed with Will's CPA. When I probed further, however, and asked why the company had lost money in the past three years, I learned that Will had been investing heavily in the research and development of a new switching device. This device could revolutionize cellular and wireless switching networks technology and was particularly applicable in the development of wireless networks, which were just beginning to emerge. Through further inquiry, I learned this technology was patentable and that Will was certain it would greatly enhance the services of his company could provide. Supporting Will's assertion was a multi-million-dollar contract from an international wireless communication technology."

Will's story shows that sometimes buyers are more interested in your proprietary protected technology than they are in your business. You may be able to sell off a protected technology by itself for cash, and still keep your *Bulletproof Business*!

Growing Cash Flow

Value Catalysts are important because they directly affect your bottom line. Buyers are looking for stability and growth in your cash flow. Most of the time, your business won't be sold for its equipment, facilities, or goodwill; it will be sold for the opportunity to enjoy future cash flows. Buyers are looking for investments and will pay top dollar for companies that look like they have rosy futures. Prior to the sale, increasing cash flow is key to achieving high offers.

Realistic Growth Strategy

Buyers pay a premium for realistic growth strategies. How is that cash flow going to grow once they take it over? Your growth strategy needs to be communicated to potential buyers in such a way that they see actual, concrete reasons that cash flow will grow after they acquire your business. Buyers will not understand your business as well as you do, so they will miss opportunities that you see, unless you point these out.

For all these reasons, Value Catalysts are a vital portion of the Bulletproof Exit Process. They preserve value, reduce risks, and enhance the final sales price. Whether you are planning on transitioning to an insider or an outsider, it is vitally important to spend time working on your Value Catalysts. In the event of an inside transfer, Value Catalysts must be in place so the transitioning owner can be fully compensated, in order to truly step aside or retire. In the event of a sale, the business will need Value Catalysts to attract buyers willing to pay top dollar.

Family Value Catalysts

The steps to family growth are different than for business growth, but the strategy is surprisingly similar. Families with generational wealth opportunities often look much like a business, with a constitution, family council, and sometimes even a family bank.

> **"Significant family wealth without the proper training to manage it can easily become a curse instead of a blessing."**

Though the structures of a successful family are important, we must remember that, the real wealth of a family is not financial. The primary assets are the family members - their unique talents, knowledge, and experience. Significant family wealth without the proper training to manage it can easily become a curse instead of a blessing, and it's likely your family will not possess that money for long.[8]

The catalysts for creating family value (what we call "financial legacy") may include:

- Estate Planning
- Asset Protection Plans
- Family Limited Partnerships/Limited Liability Companies
- Education Plans
- Donor Advised Fund/Foundations
- Dynasty Trust
- Irrevocable Life Insurance Trusts

Estate Planning

Estate planning is important for every family. Just like Value Catalysts in business, estate planning is designed to help you transfer assets to the next generation, protect your core interests, and increase the impact of your organization. Estate planning will take care of your family in the event of your death, facilitate the distribution of your property, and help to minimize estate taxes.

Asset Protection Plans

Asset protection is a pretty simple concept. It's the strategies you put in place to keep your assets away from anyone who wants to take them. Some strategies use state law inside the U.S. to accomplish the planning, while others use international trust planning systems. There is a great debate raging about which one is superior, but the important part for you to remember is to make sure it's included in your estate planning discussions.

---

8   *Family Business Alliance. Retrieved June 2014:(http://www.fbagr.org/index.php?option=com_content&view=article&id=117&Itemid=75)*

Family Limited Partnerships/Limited Liability Companies

For families whose wealth is growing and need to control risk, Family Limited Partnerships (FLPs) or Limited Liability Companies (LLCs) are essential Value Catalysts. FLPs and LLCs are incredibly beneficial instruments if they are structured correctly. They may allow a family to reduce or eliminate estate taxes, secure assets in a single entity, give parents full control of their family legacy, keep assets in the family, simplify giving, and provide protection from creditors and litigators.

It is imperative that you consult with a competent attorney when setting up an FLP or LLC. For the entity to work as designed, it needs to be run completely by the book. Your business or estate planning attorney should guide you through the rules of FLP or LLC creation and maintenance.

Education Plan

Since most of our clients will not qualify for educational aid from the government, it's important for them to diligently plan for their children's futures. There are plenty of tools available, including 529 plans, irrevocable trusts, and Uniform Gifts to Minors, also known as UGMAs (or Uniform Transfer to Minors, depending on the state you live in).

If you have children who are planning on going to college, you need to take charge of their education. It is a wonderful opportunity to teach them about return on investment, the allocation of capital, and the joys of hard work. Don't miss this time! It is not the school system's job to raise or educate your children. It is up to you to teach them how to become men and women of creativity, integrity, and diligence.

If you're looking for more in-depth understanding on how to help your children win the college game, save money, and graduate as adults, then check out the course our family created: https://wealthfit.com/courses/zero-student-debt/ to learn more!

Donor Advised Fund

For families looking for more charitable flexibility, I often recommend Donor Advised Funds (DAFs), and have one myself. They are very flexible, simple, and cheap to administer. DAFs allow donors to receive an immediate tax benefit when they place the assets into the fund, which they can direct to charities according to their prerogative over time. The donor may contribute as frequently to the fund as they would like, then grant to the charity of their choice when ready. I like DAFs for the $5-$50 million net worth client range because they allow the donor a great deal of control, but are easier and cheaper to maintain than a private foundation.

Dynasty Trust

Dynasty trusts are a foundational structure for families who desire to leave financial legacies. They can greatly reduce your family's future estate tax bill, allow you to adopt an endowment type model for your family, and help you to maintain your long-term investment horizon. Dynasty trusts let you retain much longer control over your assets than other trust models.

Irrevocable Life Insurance Trusts

For many families we work with, there is a need to hold life insurance policies in an Irrevocable Life Insurance Trust. At your death, this would prevent the proceeds of the life insurance from being included in your estate. You often hear insurance salesmen tell you that life insurance proceeds are tax free. This is only sometimes true. *If the company is paying for the life insurance and deducting it, then it will not be income tax free.* If you die owning the policy on your life, it will be subject to estate taxes to the extent you exceed your unified credit, which is the amount you can transfer at your death, estate tax free. We use the Irrevocable Life Insurance Trust in ways to mitigate these issues.

It's important to keep these Value Catalysts in mind as you plan for the inevitable transfer of your company. You won't be able to implement them all immediately, but it's imperative that you start today. Rome wasn't built in a day as they say! Value Catalysts are easily the longest step in the Bulletproof Exit Process, but they are always worth the effort because of the value they add in the end. As you can see by now, implementing this process can truly alter the course of your life, and your family's future legacy for generations. We believe that is something worth fighting for!

Action Questions:

Do you have:

- A stable and motivated management team?
- A diverse customer base?
- A nice facility appearance?
- Financial controls in place?
- Proprietary technology?
- Growth in cash flow?
- A realistic growth strategy?

Have you considered:

- Estate Planning?
- Asset Protection Plans?
- Family Limited Partnerships/Limited Liability Companies?
- Education Plans?
- Donor Advised Fund/Foundations?
- Dynasty Trusts?
- Irrevocable Life Insurance Trusts?

Chapter 6

STEP 5: Increase Business Durability

Rome, Italy, 753 B.C–1453 A.D.

The Roman Empire was a machine of brutal efficiency. At its height, the Empire was the largest political and social structure in the Western world. Rome wasn't impressive just for its breadth, however, but also for its durability. The Pax Romana, or "the Peace of Rome," ushered in a time of peace and prosperity for a 1,000 years.

Part of the reason it endured was because of how it treated those it conquered. Instead of subjecting conquered lands to mere slavery, Rome enveloped them into Roman culture. This allowed inclusion for every tribe, as long as they paid allegiance to the crown. In return, Rome gave all a government that represented the citizen voice, "The Senate and People of Rome."

In the end, Rome was built to endure. Fading away was never an option. From their military prowess to their quick-drying cement, Rome was established on the idea that Rome would never end. All Romans were born with one belief, one goal in mind: to create an Empire that would last through the ages. Anything less was less than Roman.

* * * * *

Today, American society is devoted to instant gratification. We want it all; we want it now. *But while society preaches prosperity of the moment, your business needs investment for the future.*

> " **But while society preaches prosperity of the moment, your business needs investment for the future.** "

Longevity, not short-term profitability, is the goal of The Bulletproof Exit Process. Just as a clan would take refuge in their castle for times of trouble in the feudal days, so too can a legacy family rely on a *Bulletproof Business* to help all survive through lean times.

You must make sure your business can survive without you. It's not easy to think about death, disability, or retirement, but the durability of your business depends on your answer.

Two events can easily deal crushing blows to your business's durability: (1) the loss of the owner and (2) the loss of the company's key talent.

- If you were disabled, do you have powers of attorney in place to protect the family and the business?

  If you don't have the right documents ready, your family will need court approval to make decisions about you and your business. Can you imagine the chaos that would ensue if they had to wait on the court system to fill your shoes?

- Would your management team be equipped to carry on without your guidance, reputation, and expertise?

Several years ago, we started working with a family on the East Coast that was looking to transition the business from father to son. One of the challenges was the fact that the father was running the business with a management team that was all in their 60s and 70s. He knew if he wasn't careful, the entire management team would want to retire with him, leaving his son with no one on which to rely.

Thankfully, he was looking ahead and knew something must be done. Over the course of a year or two, we worked with him and his son to bring in new blood to the management team. This time, the management team would be built around the son instead of the father. When the full transition occurred, the business didn't miss a step because the son's team was ready, in place, and firing on all cylinders.

If you have a management team that is quickly aging, it's time to look ahead and plan for the durability of your business. Transitioning a management team takes time.

Key questions to ask yourself:

- Can your business survive the loss of your key talent?
- Who brings in new business, maintains key relationships, or oversees critical operations?
- What would happen to the other employees or your customers if your talent left?

At the heart of the Bulletproof Exit Process is the idea that you can build something that outlasts you, the true definition of legacy. In fact, my favorite story of legacy family and business continuity is the Beretta Corporation.

Beretta, as you know, is the world-famous Italian small arms manufacturer. Their weapons are used by law enforcement, military, and private citizens the world over. But what you may not know is that the company has been operating since the early 16th century[9] *and* is still family owned. Beretta's succession plan is simple but elegant: In every new generation, a select few family members are groomed

---

[9] "Since 1526." *World Of Beretta*. Beretta, n.d. Web. <http://www.beretta.com/en-us/world-of-beretta/since-1526/>.

to be company officers, but every member of the family gets a share of company stock. As the family has grown, so have the company's profits. Thus, although each successive heir has received a smaller and smaller share of the total wealth, the family as a whole has continued to grow a bigger and bigger fortune.

If your goal is to have wealth that survives through generations, the Beretta family is a wonderful family to emulate. The first step is to make sure the business can survive without you and can be passed down the generations. It won't last two generations, much less dozens, if the business is built solely around your own skills. Now, your goal may not be to transfer to family members once you retire, but even if you are looking to sell, continuity is a vital ingredient to guarantee a high sales price.

Business Durability Structures

Obviously, it is important to put in place key structures to help manage the impact of tragic accidents, disabilities, or even a normal retirement. Here are the top four I believe you need to focus on:

1. Buy/Sell Agreements
2. Deferred Compensation
3. Key Employee Insurance
4. Stay Bonus

Buy/Sell Agreement

For businesses with more than a single owner, we cannot overemphasize the importance of a buy/sell agreement (or the business continuity agreement). It is one of the most important documents of your career. It ensures that your wishes are executed in case of your disability, death or the untimely departure of any shareholder. The buy/sell agreement is *the* definitive document that controls the transfer of ownership between owners in certain key situations.

I am constantly astounded at the number of businesses with multiple shareholders that do not have this basic agreement in place. Some years ago, I was brought in to help solve a problem created by the death of one of four brothers who owned a large contracting company together. Because there was no buy-sell agreement in place, the brothers could not buy out the deceased brother's spouse. In other words, they were automatically in business with their sister-in-law, who was now an equal shareholder! We finally resolved the issues, but not before she extracted a significant amount of money and emotion from her brothers-in-law and their business. A bit of advice: better to learn from their pain than experience it on your own.

Deferred Compensation

Deferred Compensation is basically a promise to pay later for work done today. The purpose is to make sure your key employees are invested in the company long-term, especially if calamity strikes. Deferred compensation is simply a written agreement between the employer and employee in which a portion of an employee's income is paid out at a later date than it was actually earned. The employee will receive it typically in retirement, assuming they meet the terms of the agreement, which may include a vesting schedule. Deferred compensation is an extra incentive for your employees to stay on in a time of crisis. The last thing you want is for people to jump ship when you need them the most.

> **The last thing you want is for people to jump ship when you need them the most.**

Key Employee Insurance

The one situation that is likely to have the most impact on your bottom line, and may challenge the very survival of your business, is the loss of your key employee(s). When the success of the entire firm depends on a small group of people, it is vital that your Bulletproof Exit Planner first identifies these individuals, then implements a plan to minimize the risk of their loss.

Usually risk mitigation involves taking out a life insurance policy (owned by the business) on each of the key employees. We normally advise making the surviving spouse of the employee a co-beneficiary of the policy. This induces the key employee to allow you to buy life insurance on his life. We typically see the surviving spouse get 10-25 percent of the policy proceeds.

Having suitable replacements already positioned inside the firm can also substantially mitigate this risk. However, if you are the only key employee, it will be almost impossible to keep the company afloat even with insurance. If you are unwilling or unable to grow your business beyond yourself, then what you really have is a job, not a *Bulletproof Business*.

Stay Bonus

As you plan for your transition, you also need to incentivize the key employees to stay past your exit, or they may leave when you need them most. You do not want key employees quitting on the eve of the sale. Nor do you want them threatening to kill your deal for a piece of the sale. Damage control is not planning, and last-minute negotiating with employees is a nightmare. Your BraveHeart Plan must facilitate the retention of key employees before, during, and after the transition, with agreements that predate the sale process.

Sometimes, when getting ready for a sale, you need to change the incentive package for top management. In April of 2011, we were brought in by a CPA firm in Florida to help a fairly large business client create a BraveHeart Plan for the owner and to provide wealth management services for his family. One of the issues we spotted during our planning was a bloated profit-sharing plan for the management team, with no goals or metrics in place.

We realized it was time to create something new. We built a bonus system for the management team in which they received a profit share once the company met a certain level of revenue. We then built another level of incentives in which management of each department could receive an extra bonus if they met certain metrics unique to their departments. Finally, we began to offer deferred compensation for the key employees, as designated by the owners, which paid a ten-year income benefit at age 65. Now we had a management team aligned with the owners' goals of growing the company!

I've also seen the ugly side of not having a plan in place. At some level, key management members will always be involved in a sale, for better or worse. For example, one particular client I worked with had a key employee who had made a significant impact on the business, but was not included in the sale process until near the end. When buyers interviewed him about his role in the company, he started to understand how valuable he was to the whole process. He threatened (and nearly succeeded) to blow up the entire sale. In the end, my client had to pay him a million dollars at closing—not exactly the way he had anticipated finishing up the sale!

Involving key people in the exit process long before buyers come to the table is enormously important. It makes key people feel valued and incentivizes them to build value into the company. It also helps owners to share some of the significant time and effort involved in the sale process when these employees are on the deal team.

Family Durability

Just to be clear, ensuring the survival of your business is only half the battle. You must also make sure that your family is prepared for risk, no matter what happens. When I take clients through The Bulletproof Exit Process, I conduct a review of their entire personal risk management strategy, insurance included. You would be surprised how often we find holes in clients' coverages!

In my experience, too many wealthy families have no one looking at the whole picture. They have their business insurance specialist cover their commercial liability, they have their attorney review their legal documents, and they have their personal insurance agent sell them coverage, but no one knows how all three work together. Over my thirty-five years of working with business owners, I'm still astounded by the gaps in coverage I continually find with my clients. Sometimes, the risk they unwittingly carry is terrifying.

One of my favorite stories involves a very successful family company, now run by the second generation. Their business coverage was near spotless. There were one or two small issues, but overall the insurance agent had done a really nice job and seemed extremely competent. However, when I reviewed the owner's personal coverage, I found an entirely different story. The next time he came to my office, I asked him a suspiciously unassuming question: "Did you go to high school with your insurance agent?" Surprised, he responded, "Yeah. How did you know that?"

I wanted to say, "Because your personal insurance coverage is a disaster," but I held my tongue. "Because it looks like you have been sold the same type of coverage you needed when you graduated high school. Only one small problem: when you bought this policy you were worth thousands, but today you are worth millions. I'm sure your insurance agent is a nice guy, but he is out of his league. You need a serious overhaul on your personal insurance."

"What do you mean?" he said. "I thought I had $10 million in liability coverage."

"Your business has $10 million in liability coverage, but you personally are extremely underinsured. Let me ask you something, do you know what would happen if your wife runs a red light and kills me?" (I know, it's a tough question, but these are the questions that must be addressed.)

He shook his head. "Honestly, I don't have a clue."

"Well, my wife would sue you for millions, and since your personal insurance only covers up to $500,000, she would most likely become a major shareholder in your company."

His jaw dropped. He could not believe it!

Just because you have good business insurance doesn't mean that you have enough insurance to cover your personal liability.

Think it can't happen to you? I had another client named Barry who owned a very large trucking company in Southern California. He came to me to do some estate planning. I started by looking over his business insurances and found that his business liability coverage was woefully inadequate. I also discovered he was running the company as a sole proprietor, when he should have been incorporated to protect him from large liability claims in the event of an accident.

I asked him, "Why are you running a trucking company in California as a sole proprietor? That makes absolutely no sense. You're personally liable for every truck you own on the road!" He told me that he had been advised by his CPA to remain a sole proprietorship because there was no tax reason to incorporate. He thought it was a waste of money.

Barry was living on the edge and didn't even know it. I told him that in California, if one of his trucks was in an accident, he could be sued for everything he had. The CPA might have known his tax work, but he was a lousy insurance agent and lawyer. We incorporated the business and bumped up his liability coverage. Providentially, we got it done just in time.

A few months later, one of Barry's trucks was involved in a horrible accident. Some steel bars broke free from the flatbed trailer and fell onto the freeway. The bars bounced on the road, up into the air, and through the windshield of the car driving behind.

The family in the car was severely impacted. The aftermath was horrible, but there were two silver linings that emerged because of our work together.

First, the family was able to use Barry's insurance money to pay for the medical bills that incurred from this horrible tragedy (the insurance company paid out to the policy limits of $10 Million). While there is no way to compensate for human loss, at least the family didn't also have to be buried under the weight of overwhelming medical bills.

Second, Barry kept his *Bulletproof Business*. If the proper insurance and legal work had not been done, the family would've been forced to sue Barry for everything he had in order to make up for their loss. In the end, despite the tragic accident, both parties benefited from proper planning. Without the planning, things would have been much worse for the two families.

Catastrophic events are terrible enough on their own. Not having the proper insurance is an injustice to the injured and may be the difference between you keeping your livelihood or losing everything. To help you avoid similar errors and risks, I have compiled some of the more common problems I find, as well as strategies to mitigate them so you can build a *Bulletproof Business*.

Personal Property Casualty Review

Families with high net worth need to conduct a property/casualty review every couple of years, especially if major changes have happened. You need someone to review both the personal and the business coverages. If you are worth a few million dollars or more, you should look for insurance brokerage firms that are able to write policies from the higher end insurance companies.

Regardless of who you use as a property/casualty broker, you should make it clear that you want them to act as a consultant, not just a salesman. As a Bulletproof Exit Planner, I like to ask the insurance brokers to give their opinion on the clients' overall risk profile. I also want to understand if my client can be successfully sued for an amount that is considerably greater than their current liability policy limits. If you can turn your insurance broker into a consultant, it will be much easier to make wise decisions regarding your insurance needs.

Personal Umbrella Policy

We strongly encourage all of our clients to own umbrella policies. Basically, an umbrella policy sits on top of your traditional business and/or personal liability insurance and only kicks in once those limits have been exceeded. It's the cheapest way to acquire additional and substantial liability insurance for your home, your vehicles, and your business. We highly recommend all higher net worth clients to make use of such a fantastic risk management tool.

Life Insurance

People tend to think that if they are relatively young and healthy, they don't have to worry about death. But the truth is, the further away you are from retirement, the more need you have to protect against premature death. Why? The risk is smaller, but the impact is higher. The younger you are, the less likely you have saved up the necessary assets to provide for your family once you are gone.

Although we do use life insurance for other purposes, its main use is to hedge against financial loss due to premature death. This allows you to provide the income your family would have had, if you had survived. Life insurance, even if its only term insurance, is a great way to make sure your family that can survive tragedy.

Vehicle Access and Insurance

Of all the insurances we review, vehicle insurance is often the most overlooked. You may not realize this but in some states, if you own the car, you may be liable for damages caused by the driver even if it's someone else!

For the average American, the car creates the greatest risk of economic loss in both property and liability damage. I remember clearly the day I learned this lesson firsthand.

I was driving to meet my wife for dinner around 5:30 pm when my client Aaron called me in a panicked voice. He said, "The cops are holding my brother out on a dirt road south of town. He's in trouble and I need your help now." I wheeled around with a pit in my stomach and told my wife we needed to postpone our dinner.

When I finally got to the scene, I realized the situation was dire. Aaron's brother, Kurt, had been driving his truck on a dirt road when a 16-year-old kid on a four-wheeler turned right in front of him, almost causing him to run off the road. Kurt had a short fuse, and the kid cutting him off made him mad. He nudged up to the back of the four-wheeler and gave the kid a little tap on the rear with his bumper.

It didn't go well from there. The impact scared the kid and made him lose control. He ran off the road and flew off his four-wheeler. He went one way and the four-wheeler went the other. It just so happened that the kid's father had driven up about the same time. As you can expect, he was furious. He called the cops and wanted to press charges for attempted murder, or at least assault with a deadly weapon.

Thankfully, his son only had a few scratches from the accident. After calming down, the dad decided not to press charges, but agreed to have Kurt do community service for one of his charities. Just like that it was over.

Now, as horrible as that story is, it could've been far worse—for both parties. Too many business owners don't realize how easy it is for their mistakes to become catastrophes. Things that start out small can involve jail time, the loss of their business, or their family's savings, if they don't have the right tools in place.

We have worked with hundreds of business owners to clean up their insurance and risk management, but there are many who refuse to look into this vital area of business continuity planning. Choose not to be one of them!

Consider Your Retirement

Even if you dodge these tragedies, your day of retirement is still approaching. If you're ready, you can look forward with great anticipation! If your business doesn't need you, and you are diversified out of your need for company income, you will enjoy immense freedom in the exit process.

> **"If your business doesn't need you, and you are diversified out of your need for company income, you will enjoy immense freedom in the exit process."**

You can take advantage of selling opportunities and remove some of the exit pressure because you don't need the sale or transition of your business to fund your full retirement. The beauty of preparing so far in advance is that BraveHearts are able to decide the exact date, time, and successor for their *Bulletproof Business*.

Action Questions:

- Could the business survive if you were disabled?
- Would the business survive the loss of your key talent?
- When is the last time you've had someone review all your insurance coverages?

CHAPTER 7

STEP 6: Live Your Legacy

Over thousands of years only one people group has kept their roots and their heritage intact even after losing their country in 70 A.D. Weaving in and out of world events, disappearing into the tapestry of world culture, the distinct thread of the Jewish people has remained for centuries.

The ancient Egyptians made slaves of the Jews, the Assyrians shut them up like "a bird in a cage", and the Babylons exiled many of their people after destroying the temple. Over the centuries they have been thrown into ghettos and suffered under many pogroms. Characterized as greedy, miserly, and controllers of the world's financiers, many have sworn to stamp them out. In WWII Hitler boldly declared, "The result of this war will be the complete annihilation of the Jews." More than six million were killed. But none have succeeded in their quest to eliminate them. Time and time again, when hope seemed all but lost, the Jewish people have survived.

For millennia, their culture, faith, and even their resourcefulness have stood the test of time. Despite intense persecution, a lack of country to call their own, and cruel annihilation tactics by some of the world's governments, they remained. And in 1949, their nation was restored! This kind of thing has never happened before. Today the Jewish network worldwide is astounding, their connections to one another strong, and their legacy enduring. Currently residing in 135 countries, 97 have permanent organizations in order to maintain their Jewish community, retaining the bonds of legacy and culture.

* * * * *

The Jewish people embody the term "legacy." They have held onto their history, heritage, faith, and family identity through thousands of years of persecution and dispersion. What started out as a family of sheepherders in the middle of the desert, has become one of the most influential people groups in history. Talk about leaving a legacy!

> "
> ## A family is much like a business: if it is not growing, it is dying. "

Creating a legacy is at the heart of the Bulletproof Exit Process. Family matters! Legacy is not something that you can save until later. You must begin now. A family is much like a business: if it is not growing, it is dying. Family is at the focus of the Bulletproof Exit Process because if you get this wrong, it doesn't matter how well the rest of the process goes.

You will not be remembered for the size of your balance sheet, but rather the impact you make on people and the legacy you leave through your children and your employees. Everyone, regardless of the size of his bank account, has a chance to leave a legacy. The only thing holding you back is the amount of work you are willing to put in. Your success in creating a family legacy is directly proportional to how well you plan, prepare, and execute the legacy building process.

"Legacy building" is the process that creates heirs who regularly contribute to the financial, human, intellectual, and social capital of their families and community; who are connected to their extended families and work hard to maintain positive family relations, effective communication, and generational growth; who count their blessings and embrace their responsibility to love their neighbors and give more than they receive; and who develop the competencies to handle the responsibilities of wealth and effectively utilize the opportunities that they have been handed.

A business owner who builds a successful legacy doesn't have a family that simply relies on him and his wealth, but rather builds things of their own, such as their own families, careers, businesses, arts, or charities. It is my experience that too many business owners try to build a successful business instead of a successful family. But not Legacy Families. These families refuse to be owned by their wealth. Instead, they put it to work to make a difference in their families, their communities, and the world at large.

Henry Jones is the head of one of my favorite Legacy Families. When he was in his late 40s, Henry and his wife lost everything they had due to a joint venture that went bad. Rather than give up, the Joneses stayed together and worked to rebuild over the following years, even though the financial loss wasn't their fault. Henry was able to rebuild so successfully that the family wealth far surpasses what he lost, with business in the U.S. and two foreign countries. Today, he enjoys a thriving legacy that will continue for generations. The road was hard, but Henry and his wife persevered when lesser men and women would have quit.

Henry and his wife have exhibited such a love for each other that many envy their happiness. But few know the hard road they have traveled. In the midst of those hard times, they taught their children the joys of hard work and the blessing of perseverance. They imprinted the ideas of faith and family legacy on their children from a young age. The children grew up working alongside their parents, learning the family business, and how to raise a family. And though they are financially successful, it is clear that the real wealth of the family is founded on genuine affection for each other and an abiding faith in our Lord Jesus Christ.

Their children are continuing the family legacy by exposing the grandchildren to the same kind of experiences and teaching. They are investing their time, talents, and finances into the next generation without forgetting the most important part to them: their faith.

So how does one build a family that remains profitable, successful, healthy, loving and content, for not just one, but many generations? How does one ensure that the family has not only money, but also connection, compassion, and competency?

The key to having a family like this is to raise children in a positive environment where unconditional love is freely given, faith in God is taught and modeled, and forgiveness is practiced. While we all make mistakes and fail to live up to our potential, it is important to do our best and to encourage our children to do their best as well.

Now, this isn't to say that perfect parenting will solve all your problems (as if there were such a thing!)

Just last year, I counseled a dentist who was broken-hearted over his daughter caught in a life of drug addiction. He had done everything "right." He was an honorable man, well respected, and he had raised three beautiful children with a clear knowledge of right and wrong. But during college, one of his daughters began experimenting with drugs and became trapped in that lifestyle. It became a living nightmare for the man and his wife.

The daughter is about 50 now and is still caught up in that world. As you can imagine, her lifestyle choices have caused continued conflict between the dentist and his wife. One wants to cut the daughter off, and the other wants to make sure she doesn't become homeless. Further complicating the situation, a granddaughter is also caught in the middle of it all.

I tell you this story as an important caveat: Regardless of how well you train up your children, they must still make their own choices, so be sure to balance your personal responsibility with teaching them how to make decisions. Let them make some age appropriate decisions for which they succeed or suffer the consequences of failure. Better to learn while the stakes are small.

> **Building a family of wealth instead of just a wealthy family is a mission worth pursuing.**

That being said, if you start today you will go a long way towards building a family legacy that lasts. It is never too late to make the ones you love a priority. *Building a family of wealth instead of just a wealthy family is a mission worth pursuing.* The rewards include rich and loving relationships as well as productive descendants for generations. Those who choose to accept this mission will find it requires intentional planning, lots of hard work, and a willingness to risk it all in order to win it all. But the rewards far outweigh the effort!

Action Steps

- Find a way to incorporate your children into the business.
- Teach them how to make decisions and manage their own finances.
    — If you are interested in learning more, check out our family's finance course for young adults: https://wealthfit.com/courses/financial-adulting/
- Embody love, forgiveness, and wisdom in your interactions.

CHAPTER 8

Transition to Family

London, England 1170 A.D.

Romanticized by his people and minstrels alike, Richard the Lionheart was larger than life. Standing over 6'5, with red-gold hair, blue eyes, and bulging muscles, he had the disciplined body of a champion fighter and the keen mind of a skilled commander. Richard had a reputation for military prowess and fearlessness that bordered on foolishness. His foremost foe, Saladin of Egypt, respected him greatly, and even sent him two replacements when he lost his horse in battle.

He put down a rebellion in Gascony, conquered the island of Sicily, captured the town of Acre, and almost retook Jerusalem, but he is perhaps best known for his role in the Robin Hood legend. Richard was loved by his people and respected by his enemies.

But his family hated each other.

In 1170, Richard's father, King Henry II decided to divide his kingdom between his three eldest surviving sons: Henry, Richard, and Geoffrey. However, King Henry II still retained ultimate control over his possessions, including the all-important purse strings. Henry's motivation for splitting up his kingdom while he was alive remains a mystery. He may have wanted to slow down as he got older or perhaps give his sons limited leadership experience under his protection. No matter the intent, the plan did not work.

Henry's sons became disenchanted with the status quo almost immediately after the division. They chafed under their father's heavy-handed control. Not content to wait for their father's death, all three sons rose up in rebellion to take the kingdom from King Henry II while he was still alive.

Henry II responded with speed, brutality, and overwhelming force. He quickly crushed the rebellion, forcing his sons to beg for forgiveness and sue for peace. Henry spared their lives, but took away most of their land. In a peculiar move of cruelty, Henry forced his son Richard to punish the barons that had joined him in the rebellion. Richard eventually found some semblance of peace with his father, but the infighting and political intrigue would continue amongst the family for the rest of their lives. Even the brothers who fought alongside each other soon turned against each other.

It wasn't until Richard's brothers died that he became King of England.

* * * * *

Henry II might have raised a Lionheart, but he was no BraveHeart. In a family business, in-fighting can destroy the business and the family! It isn't enough to fight *for* each other; you have to fight *together* for something that lasts. King Henry infuriated his allies, impoverished his kingdom, and destroyed his family relations. The lesson to learn: You can make a lot of money, but if you lose the succession battle, your family's success can easily end with you.

> **It isn't enough to fight for each other; you have to fight together for something that lasts.**

Succession disputes have caused more wars and pain than perhaps any other single event. Henry II's poor planning and heavy-handed leadership style sparked a rebellion and almost cost him a kingdom. Planning ahead, managing leadership transition, and knowing who is in charge will go a long way toward maintaining order and profitability in your business.

I have been a part of countless transitions in my career. Sometimes, the family transitions are the most difficult to pull off successfully. You'd think that transitioning to like-minded individuals who love each other, and work with you, would be simple, but it rarely is. *You have to wade through family conflict, emotions, sentiments, and all the mess that comes with being a family on top of all the financial, legal, tax, and cash flow issues of a pure business transition.*

Transitioning your business to your children or other family members is not simply a matter of finances or tax savings. Your family may maintain professionalism in their work, but when the time for your exit arrives, it can be a whole new ball game. Not only does your exit bring up new issues to fight over, but it can also reveal underlying conflicts.

Family conflicts can derail the entire transition process. The key to smoothing relationships and maintaining transition momentum is understanding that the problem being talked about is rarely the real issue. *Business families have the tendency to suppress problems in the name of professionalism and "keeping the peace."* Unfortunately, changes that set an entirely new course for the business are bound to open old wounds. Your exit has the potential to turn into a power struggle, no matter how much your family members love and respect each other.

It's imperative to keep the end in mind and to be ready for the issues that will come. Transitioning to outsiders is hard enough; managing family relations can add even more confusing components to the mix.

Family Leadership Transitions

Once you've decided to leave the business to your family, there are many options. The level of sophistication and preparation varies, so keep in mind your unique family situation as you think through the possibilities. As with all things in the Bulletproof Exit Process, it's important to plan and follow through. Some ways are naturally better than others, but in general, there are five common ways family business owners exit.

1) Baptism By Fire

With this method, the CEO maintains control until some unfortunate set of events forces him to suddenly relinquish the reins. The successor is then forced to immediately assume complete and total control with little preparation. It's sink or swim! Usually this is a poor way to transition, but it does have one advantage: The family does not have to endure the conflicts that so often accompany a phased transition while the leader is letting go and the successor is acquiring more responsibility.

The downside to Baptism by Fire is the successor is suddenly thrust into a leadership position for which they are often ill-equipped. Some successors will bear the burden and manage to survive against the odds, but many will fail. If your desire is to leave your business to your children, it is much better to help them develop their leadership skills before your exit. The chances of them succeeding are much higher if they have the opportunity to acquire experience and fail in small ways before assuming the full weight of responsibility.

2) Mañana Motion

Many leaders are wary of leaving cold turkey so they delay, delay, delay. I call it the "Mañana Motion" (as in "leaving tomorrow!"). The delay game really doesn't have any advantages. Instead, it frustrates any potential successors, making them bitter and a potential flight risk. Delaying does not inspire the kind of legacy our firm wants for your family.

Whenever a *mañana* leader finally dies or hands the reins over, the successor may be so used to following that he doesn't want to lead. The best example I can think of was one of our California clients, Bob. The day Bob turned 80, he decided it was time to hand over the reins to his daughter. When Bob finally let her know that he was ready to exit and the business was all hers, she looked at him and said, "Dad, are you serious? I'm 60, *I'm* planning on retiring this year!"

Leadership needs to be developed by slowly giving increasing responsibility to the successor while teaching them along the way. I have had many clients who managed the gradual transition wonderfully, Mark being a prime example.

Mark is one of my clients who owns a large plumbing business. He's been grooming his son, Julian, for the past 25 years to take the business over. Julian started working in the field as a support person for the plumbers when he was in high school, and after college, he came back to the family business to make it his life's work. After ten years of training and helping the business grow, Julian was given a substantial ownership stake in the business.

Mark retired a few years ago, and Julian, who now owns 40 percent, runs the business and has doubled its size within the last five years. Mark has plans in place to transition the rest of the business to Julian at his death. Julian's siblings, who chose not to work in the business, have been provided for through Mark's personal assets and insurance. This is a good example of someone who made a plan, developed the management skills in his son, and has preserved the family relationships by dealing with the process in an open manner with the rest of the family.

3) The Cat Came Back

I call this tactic, "The Cat Came Back" because the leader turns over control very quickly, hops on a plane or boat for an extended vacation, and then suddenly returns to reassert control. The leader may periodically retreat to a seasonal residence or take a sabbatical, but at the end of their trip they always show up back at the business. When the past leader returns, they usually change initiatives and projects that have been implemented in their absence. Some owners never even bother to change titles when they return, preferring to be the absentee master and commander.

The Cat Came Back is probably the most destructive of the transition strategies. While the successor does gain some experience—and transition does occur temporarily—the Here, Gone, Here, Gone gambit may cause the successor to become fed up and leave. Key employees are also tempted to leave, as they are pulled in two directions. No one likes to be placed in the middle of a conflict. What is even more discouraging for the employees is to see the initiatives they have worked so hard on undermined or removed by the reappearing leader who can't seem to let go.

4) Transition CEO

The fourth option is to place into position a non-family CEO. I call this the "Transition CEO." In this case, the owner transfers control to someone outside the family while the owner gradually withdraws over the next five-to-ten years. The non-family CEO then mentors the successor until the CEO retires. This option is a clear win for families who have successors clearly interested in running the business, but not quite ready to be handed the reins. It also allows the interim CEO to help train the successor to develop the skills needed to be the next family leader. A bonus is that a respected non-family leader can introduce new skills to the business and implement needed innovations and changes much more easily than a green successor could.

5) The Wise Approach

The final transition strategy is the Gradual/Progressive approach, or what I would call the "Wise Approach." As is obvious from my moniker, this method is my favorite. *With the Wise Approach, you gradually cede more and more responsibility to your successor. Somewhere between years two and five, you will be completely unnecessary to the future staying power of the business, at which point you step aside.*

If you would still like to be involved, some owners will adopt a "chairman" or "consultant" role while the successor runs the business as CEO. The advantage to this tactic is the successor gains experience gradually, using the time to absorb the lessons of leadership. Plus, with fewer responsibilities, you will be able to explore the options for your next stage of life.

The downside to the gradual approach is that there are plenty of opportunities for conflict and tension. As authority is handed over one responsibility at a time, there is potential for friction and impatience on both sides. You may also feel like you are getting pushed aside, while your successor may feel coddled or constrained.

Despite the downsides, I believe the gradual transition is the right choice for most family businesses. Leaving "cold turkey" is asking for failure. The non-family CEO approach works well, but requires just the right person. The Manana Method and The Cat Came Back approaches both can be disastrous. In my experience, allowing the successor to grow into their role is a great way for him or her to truly learn how to be an effective executive. That being said, you cannot simply designate a successor and expect the individual to learn everything on his own. Too many family businesses give the successor a broad title like executive vice president and then let them drift through their career without assuming authority over anything. A better way is giving the successor new responsibilities one by one, by a process of preparation.

Preparing the Successor

Publicly traded companies understand the pitfalls to successor transitions and take great pains to be ready. They run senior management candidates through an extensive and often exhausting selection process. The process to select a leader for a family business needs to be just as thorough, for the stakes are just as high. When a public company executive fails, people lose their jobs and investors lose their money. When a family business executive fails, the family itself is threatened. With so much at stake, it is more important than ever to institute a successor-training program with the following steps.

1) Start with Employment

The next leader of a family business needs to know the business inside and out in order to gain buy-in from key stakeholders. In a trade business, that means working their way from the ground up, learning what it takes to do each and every job in the company.

Your successor's training should cover the importance of each and every department. If he or she has worked their way up in one department and is already managing it, you may want to consider sending them back down to receive bottom level training in the other departments. You will also need to assign mentors or managers to train him or her at each level. If you do it right, by the time your successor takes over the company, he or she will know it better than you.

2) Maintain Accountability

If you are going to have family members work in your business, you need to lay out some ground rules. Will you give all interested family members a job at your company? Or will there be certain stipulations they have to meet first? Many families outline the job application procedure on paper so that it is fair and equitable for all family members and employees.

Once your potential successor gets a job in your company, you must also have a system in place to keep them accountable. However, this system needs to be objective and handled carefully. *Performance evaluations can easily feel like personal attacks, and substandard results often occur. To keep this from happening, many family businesses require family employees to report to a non-family manager.*

3) Compensate Accordingly

Once the right accountability is in place, appropriate and commensurate compensation is vital. *Family businesses tend to fall off the wagon on one of two sides: they either over-compensate family members merely because of their status as relatives, or they undercompensate family members with the rationale that the business will eventually belong to them anyway.* Both ideas are dangerous. If you overcompensate, nonfamily employees become resentful and may even leave. If you undercompensate, family members will become resentful and leave or just work with a bad attitude. The pay grade should be fair whether an employee is a part of the family or not. It's always helpful to ask, "What would this job earn in the marketplace?"

Award Appropriately

Speaking of compensation, if pay should be fair, then so should ownership. Long before your transition, you need to decide if ownership should be gifted to family employees or if they need to buy in. Some families give ownership to family regardless of if they work in the business, while others gift the business to family employees and leave passive assets to the other family members.

As a side note, if you desire to give ownership to kids that don't work in the business, consider recapitalizing the company stock by creating voting and non-voting shares. We suggest you give the non-voting stock to those who do not work in the company. Of course, seek good counsel to help you make this decision.

If you are struggling to pick a successor, a standardized training program can actually make the decision much easier. By starting early and training potential successors as you go, you will be able to simultaneously separate any disinterested heirs and equip the committed ones. Over time, it will become clear who is best suited to run the company based on their track record. If one clear heir apparent doesn't emerge, treat this as a blessing in disguise. Instead of one committed family member to rely on, your business will rest on the shoulders of a committed core. I've even known some families who have spun off different segments of their main business into standalone side businesses that each child now runs.

Training a successor is a vital part of the Bulletproof Exit Process; much like the rest of the process, the sooner you start, the better. Remember, retirement doesn't always happen when you expect it. Begin the process of transitioning your business long before you actually leave. The best exit plans start seven to ten years before the actual sale or succession. Thinking that you will get to it eventually, or the transition will work itself out, is a recipe for failure.

" Be prepared for the unthinkable. "

Make sure you have accurately assessed the risks and accounted for them. Just this year, one of my friends died of a heart attack at age 60. Today, his son runs a business he didn't think he would run for 10 to 15 years. In life, you just never know. *Be prepared for the unthinkable.* There is no perfect formula for timing a transition or creating a succession plan. Every business is different, but the key to success in any situation is to seize opportunity and manage risk. You must understand your own family situation and the business environment around you. Whatever your situation warrants, I hope you recognize that the sooner you build a *Bulletproof Business*, the better!

Action Questions:

- Do you have any children interested in the business?
- Are they on a track to learn the business?
- Are you underpaying or overpaying them?
- Are you slowing handing off responsibility and decision-making to them?

CHAPTER 9

Sale to Employees

Athens, Greece 356 B.C – 323 B.C.

At the tender age of 16, Alexander the Great began a military career that would consume the rest of his life. His first victory came after overcoming the revolting Thracians, only to quickly move on to help his father conquer Greece. After his father's death, Alexander attacked the Persian Empire, personally leading his elite calvary to victory over King Darius. For the first time in history, the Persian army was defeated with their king on the battlefield.

Shortly thereafter, the entire Persian Empire fell to Alexander's hands. Yet despite his success, his ambition could not be sated. He pushed into India, ever seeking to conquer the edges of the world. It was there, thousands of miles from home, that his loyal men finally mutinied, refusing to march any further. Alexander reluctantly agreed to turn back, but the campaign would cost him his life. He died of sickness on his way home at the age of 32.

Alexander the Great is perhaps the most successful military commander in history. Tutored by one of the greatest minds the world has ever seen, raised by a mighty king, given command of a battle-hardened army, and driven by an internal fire unparalleled by mortal men, Alexander had every element necessary for success. He overthrew the most powerful empire in existence. He was undefeated in battle. For ten straight years he never lost a fight. His empire reached from

Greece to Egypt and east all the way to India.

Yet, for all his greatness, his empire died with him. At his death, his four top generals divided the empire between them and headed their separate ways. Thus, in one fell swoop, his empire was severed into quarters.

* * * * *

Alexander's belief in his own greatness caused him to disregard succession planning. He had no obvious or legitimate heir, and he had no plans to transition control of his empire. According to legend, when Alexander was asked on his deathbed to whom he bequeathed his kingdom, his reply was "to the strongest." *His laissez faire answer to the future of his empire began forty years of civil war that resulted in the murder of his family and closest friends.*

Alexander had no children, so it was impossible for a family transition to occur, but that doesn't mean he shouldn't have thoughtfully passed down his legacy. If you are in a similar position, or have children that aren't interested in running the business, it may make sense to consider transitioning to an employee instead. Insider transactions often involve rewarding a long-time and loyal employee, while still enabling the owner to take money off the table for family and retirement purposes.

Remember that no matter how your transition is structured, it will still be a failure if it doesn't accomplish these three primary objectives:

- Transfer to whom you want
- When you want
- For the price you want

The question is this, how do you attain those objectives when your employee does not have enough cash to buy you out? Banks may provide part of the solution, but generally they want to see a track record of the employee running the company for some time or substantial funding outside of the bank loan. Since it is unlikely that your employee has a significant source of wealth outside of your business, the cash the employee needs to buy the business will need to come from the company. I know that may sound crazy, but it works in the right circumstances.

Because of the challenges inherent in an insider transition, it's important to follow a process for effective insider sales. The first step is to eventually have the new owners replace you in the business operations. That doesn't mean you just hand over the reins and then ride off into the sunset; it does mean you will need to slowly transition out of leadership. It must become the responsibility of the proposed new owners to plan to run the business, or at least create a team that will. This is the period where they prove they can manage.

Transferring Interest

The next step involves slowly transferring ownership interest without losing control. This step is critical to do correctly; you don't want to transfer control of the company until you have taken enough chips off the table. We like our clients to do this in a series of steps, like slowly gifting the stock once certain milestones are met, or selling them the minority interest in blocks over time.

Again, you should establish objective standards for your potential successor to meet before transferring the balance of the stock. These objectives can include the receipt of purchase money, release of your personal liability exposure, the payoff of business debt, etc.

Remember, no matter how much you trust your employees or co-owners, you should always have a buy-back agreement that allows you to reacquire all of the transferred ownership if certain events transpire or certain criteria are not met. For example, your employee can't make the payments on time or he is making decisions that are detrimental to the company's success. Far too many business owners hand off their businesses too early and then have to step back into a failing company when the transition doesn't work out like they planned.

The final step is to transfer control when, and only when, all of your ownership objectives have been met. Before you can do that (or even begin the process), you have to assess the readiness of your insiders.

> **The final step is to transfer control when, and only when, all of your ownership objectives have been met.**

Assess Insider Readiness

I know we've said this before, but be careful about assuming that insiders actually want to buy your business.

In July of 2013, we were hired to plan for what was supposed an insider sale for a fertilizer and chemical company. The owner, Charlie, intended to have his long-time employee, Fernando, buy the company. After the first few months of work, it was time to sit down with Fernando to explore how the transition might work.

However, when we introduced the plan to Fernando, he said, "Thank you so much for this opportunity and the trust you have in me to make this offer. However, I intend to retire and go back to Mexico to be with my family." Turns out Fernando had been investing his money into a nice place for him and his wife to retire near his family in Mexico. Now it was time for Charlie to pivot and look for another option for his transition plan.

Sometimes your transition plan will encounter unexpected twists! It is so important to lay the groundwork well in advance so that no matter what happens, you will be prepared. The key to an insider transfer is to structure the deal in such a way that the tax consequences are minimized for everyone involved, and your rights to cash flow are protected.

Understanding Cash

Remember that in an insider transition, the cash needed to purchase the initial buy-in of the insiders must often come from the business.

Unfortunately, there is an inherent problem. You own the business, and therefore you own the cash flows. If you use current cash flow to fund your transition, you are essentially buying yourself out and giving away your company for free.

So how do you take some chips off the table? First, by understanding the risk/reward ratio. The sooner you get your cash, the less risk you have. If you decide to defer payment over a number of years, you increase the risk that you may not get your full payout. In other words, If the business goes belly up in five years, but your payments were scheduled to be over ten years, you may only receive half of the purchase price.

One of the ways to reduce the risk is to take a sufficient amount of money out of the business as you go along. If you know that you are going to sell to an insider, it makes sense to take more money out of the business leading up to the sale.

Owners often keep too much money inside the business by underpaying themselves and reinvesting into the business. But waiting to get your money at the end can create a burden for the business, not to mention the tax complications. The IRS may consider it "unreasonable compensation," especially if you are a C Corp, and tax it as a dividend (which is not deductible by the business) and therefore create a taxable event for you.

One way to get around that is to transition the first 30-40 percent of the company during which time your employee builds a track record of good management. After running the company for several years, the employee can borrow the balance from the bank and pay you off, completing the sale. This is the method most often used by us because we do not let our clients transfer control of the business until their risk is off the table.

Lower Value

When selling to an insider, keep in mind that some of your goals will be different than if you were selling to a third party. For example, in a third-party sale, you want to maximize the value of the business so that you receive more money once the sale goes through. But when selling to an insider, you want to decrease the value of the business so you aren't paying more in taxes. Obviously, these are general rules and you need to consult your accountant on your specific situation, but it's important to keep these in mind as you walk down the path to an insider sale.

If you want a successful transition to your key people, you must prepare well for it. You want to do well for yourself and your family and you want to make sure the transition protects the jobs of your employees. This is a duty of stewardship to your family and your employees. Think through the necessary steps to implement along the way; a transition to an insider most often takes longer to pull off than a third-party sale.

In Alexander the Great's story, he had control over the known world and had the opportunity to save the empire and protect his people. Instead, he set his country up for disaster by deciding to delay his planning. Moral of the story? Do better.

Just like any other piece of the Bulletproof Exit Process, you need to start early if you want to make a successful transition! The sooner you plan and make decisions, the better.

Action Steps

- Have you identified a successor?
- Are they running the company now? Are they being trained to take over?
- Have you asked them if they want to buy the business?
- Do you have a good CPA to help you work through the tax implications?

CHAPTER 10

Sale to Third Party

Paris, France June 28th, 1919

The evening sun sparkled through the room, beams reflecting off row upon row of mirrors. The scene usually invoked a sense of splendor and majesty, but the mood was little matched by the defeated German commanders sitting before it. Across the table sat the arrogant French, the inflexible English, and the Johnny-come-lately Americans. Bristling with humiliated pride and national defeat, the generals of the once vaunted German Military read Article 231:

"The Allied and Associated Governments affirm and Germany accepts the responsibility of Germany and her allies for causing all the loss and damage to which the Allied and Associated Governments and their nationals have been subjected as a consequence of the war imposed upon them by the aggression of Germany and her allies."

With the signing of the Treaty of Versailles, it appeared the German aggression was finally over. The Allies had won. They drove hard bargains, threatening to resume hostilities should the Germans refuse to sign the document as is. They were able to extract large concessions from the Germans that included war reparations of 132 billion marks (which would be roughly $450 billion in today's dollars), a demilitarized Rhineland buffer zone between France and Germany, and control of former German territories by the League of Nations. It was the perfect coup de grace, or so the Allies thought.

The Treaty of Versailles officially ended World War One, but at the same time, it sowed the seeds for World War Two. The German people considered the treaty to be a national humiliation and they groaned under the harsh terms of the agreement. The necessity of paying back enormous reparations caused the Germans to devalue their currency, plunging the country into even deeper economic straits.

It was this pain and suffering on which Hitler capitalized, enabling him to seize total power. If the Allies had considered the long-term implications of the treaty, and not just the short-term financial wins, they may have avoided a Second World War altogether.

* * * * *

Negotiation for the sale of your company requires wisdom. You must thoroughly understand your position and what you truly want. What you negotiate will likely have long term consequences for you, your family, and your employees. Waiting until you are ready to leave your business does not leave you time to exit well, especially when you are selling to a third party.

History has many examples of business sale woes, but my favorite story is the napkin agreement between Andrew Carnegie and J.P. Morgan. At the time of the sale, these two were America's greatest tycoons. J.P. Morgan was looking to expand into the steel and railroad world, and over lunch asked Andrew Carnegie if he was interested in selling his company. Carnegie thought about it for a moment, did some calculations in his head, and wrote down how much he wanted on the back of a napkin and passed it to J.P Morgan. J.P. couldn't believe his good fortune and agreed without hesitation. As soon as the papers were drawn up and signed, Carnegie became one of the richest men in the world. He was pretty pleased with himself.

Out of pure curiosity, Carnegie asked J.P. how high he would have been willing to go in order to obtain the Carnegie business empire.

J.P. Morgan replied that he would have paid double and still gotten a bargain! Now, I don't know how much an extra $480 million meant to the richest man in the world back then, but isn't it sad that one of the most successful men in history didn't even know the value of his own company?

Whether you sell for a $480 million or a $100 thousand, you want to sell for a price that is a proper reflection of your company's value and provides you with the resources to live the life of your dreams.

In order to do that well, it's helpful to walk through the following nine steps in the Bulletproof Sale Process:

1. Understand the Business Sale Cycle
2. Assess Company and Owner for Sale Readiness
3. Presale Due Diligence
4. Identify Competitive Advantage
5. Identify Potential Buyers
6. Controlled Auction
7. Sale Documents
8. Closing
9. Adjusting Post Sale Expectations

The Business Sale Cycle

The first thing you need to do before you even consider putting the wheels in motion for a sale is to analyze the external business environment. What is the interest rate for financing businesses? How much private equity money is available to drive demand across the nation? Choosing the right time to exit based on the macro-environment is a good first step to getting the highest price possible.

Your business is worth the price that you can get for it, but the price you receive is directly impacted by the availability and pricing of financing. If buyers can't secure the funds to buy your business, then the amount a buyer will pay will be substantially reduced. The Mergers & Acquisitions market is directly affected by the overall health of the economy. As enthusiasm rises and economic activities pick up, more buyers will be looking to expand through acquisitions.

> " **Your business is worth the price that you can get for it, but the price you receive is directly impacted by the availability and pricing of financing.** "

Sale Readiness

Once you have examined the market, it is time to become introspective and assess your own readiness to sell. Since you have walked through the majority of the Bulletproof Exit Process already, this is going to be the easy part for you. You have already solidified your personal objectives: i.e. you know when you want to sell, to whom you want to sell, and how much money you will need from the transaction to reach your goals. You have already established a professional value estimation for your business as well as your exit goals, strategy, family considerations, advisors, and Value Catalysts.

At this point, you will also need to factor in competitors, potential buyers, industry acquisition activity, and your own competitive advantage.

Presale Due Diligence

No matter the size of the transaction, due diligence is a part of every sale. Buyers will delve into every single business record they can get their hands on to decide if your company is worth the risk and the capital invested. Due diligence can be a daunting proposition for owners looking to sell, because it involves collecting and organizing a substantial amount of information.

To combat the emotional fatigue and the grueling workload associated with due diligence, you should conduct your own internal presale due diligence first. Think of it as a dress rehearsal. It will help give you a small taste of what you will endure later, so that you will be prepared when the time comes. Additionally, it's helpful for you to take a devil's advocate approach to your business. What will a buyer think? If you can step back and look at your company with the eyes of a buyer, it will help to align your expectations with reality.

> **" If you can step back and look at your company with the eyes of a buyer, it will help to align your expectations with reality. "**

Keep in mind that buyers will do everything they can to depress the sale price. If there is a chance they can get it cheaper, they are going to try! *You can expect that any inconsistency they find, any small weakness, will be exploited. Presale due diligence allows you the chance to spot these irregularities before the buyer does, so you can be prepared for negotiations.* When it comes to negotiation, preparation is half the battle.

Competitive Advantage

You need to be clear on your company's competitive advantage. Owners who can clearly articulate why their customers prefer their *Bulletproof Business* will have an enormous advantage at the bargaining table. Knowing exactly what makes your company unique gives you a solid footing to negotiate for a superior price. By focusing on what makes your company valuable, you are sticking to what matters in the minds of buyers.

Make sure you know what sets you apart from the pack before you head to market! Anyone who is not able to communicate this advantage puts himself at an immediate disadvantage when it comes to competing for buyers and negotiating a sale.

Potential Buyers

It's important to know the type of buyer who might sit across the negotiating table from you. In most cases, there are two types of buyers: financial buyers and strategic buyers.

Financial buyers acquire businesses in order to grow them and sell them, much like real estate investors flip houses. They buy based on a financial formula that is usually some form of return on equity. A classic example of a financial buyer is a private equity group. Because it's a numbers game for them; they may even buy businesses in industries in which they only have a moderate amount of experience.

In other words, sellers will have to spend more time educating financial buyers on their processes, competitive advantage, etc., during the due diligence process. Generally, financial buyers are looking for the exit potential even as they buy. Pulling the trigger for these buyers depends solely on the opportunity to inject capital into a business they can turn around and sell for a profit within a reasonable timeframe.

Strategic buyers, on the other hand, often buy to augment their existing holdings. Thus, they are looking for synergies between their current operations and yours. They want to leverage their own market distribution, name recognition, or proprietary technology through your business assets in order to outperform what you could have done on your own. Often, strategic buyers are your competition, or someone in your supply chain.

Once you have identified all the potential buyers in your network, area, supply chain, and circles, your team will begin to gather intelligence on them. Your advisers will look into their past acquisitions, prices paid, changes in strategic acquisitions plans, problems they may be encountering, changes in industry position or reputation, personnel changes, or changes in the regulatory environment.

Controlled Auction

Once you have conducted all of the presale preparations, you are ready to execute. The two main sale options are a competitive auction (sometimes called controlled auction) and a negotiated sale. As the name implies, in a competitive auction, multiple qualified buyers bid simultaneously to purchase a company. A negotiated sale, on the other hand, involves only two parties: the buyer and the seller. In my experience, a competitive auction is the superior method because the negotiated sale tilts the scales in favor of the buyer. It's simple: The more offers you get, the more leverage you have to get a good price.

> " It's simple: The more offers you get, the more leverage you have to get a good price. "

Many owners end up in a negotiated sale, not because they necessarily want to be there, but because they get trapped. What tends to happen is that the seller unexpectedly receives an offer from a qualified strategic buyer and the seller enlists the aid of an investment banker, lawyer, or CPA to help negotiate the deal.

In this scenario, the seller has handicapped themselves from the start. Skilled buyers know they can generally purchase the business for a cheaper price, if there is no competition. Once the seller is pulled into the process, they tend to want to get a deal done and will be reluctant to walk away in the end. The money and time spent in the process is so great, the owner will usually end up taking a less than satisfactory price to finish the deal. In other words, if you cannot maintain walk-away power, your leverage has been substantially undermined, and the buyer will take advantage of that scenario.

A controlled auction, on the other hand, comes with a variety of benefits. First, it allows a pool of buyers to be involved in the process, which gives you an enormous advantage by forcing them to compete against one other. This is the chance for true price discovery. Having firms compete for your company tilts the negotiating power in your favor.

An auction also allows the seller to consider several different offers in order to pick the one that best meets his objectives, beyond the price. It helps by also minimizing risk because you will have several back up offers in case the main buyer drops out. Finally, your advisors will be able to bring buyers to the table that you haven't even considered! Overall, we think a controlled auction is the smartest way to sell your business, though you will generally need to have a company worth five million or more to entice an investment banker to represent you for a controlled auction.

Sale Documents

Every sale is going to come with a host of documents, some more important than others. Understanding each document, and its strengths and limitations, will aid you in your negotiation. I can't stress enough how important it is to have an experienced M&A lawyer. Documents often hide ticking time bombs that have the potential to blow up long after all the papers are signed. Buyers also love to hide behind confusing language, so you need an attorney who will negotiate for you and pour through the documents with you, looking for any underhanded deal points.

Closing

In the closing stage, it is imperative that you do not let your guard down. The transaction is far from over. Closing involves the most crucial moments of the entire deal. Remember that nothing is over until *all* your money is in the bank (which can happen six months to several years *after* the closing date), so be prepared to keep up the momentum and the pressure on the deal.

We managed the sale of a software company in the Southeast for a client named Henry. We picked an M&A firm to represent the company, and hired a law firm to handle the sales contract and some of the negotiation process. We spent eight months on preparation, marketing, and pairing potential buyers down to one. After 60 days of due diligence, we went with a private equity buyer offering $1 million dollars above the rest of the other offers. Everything went wonderfully … until the day before we were supposed to close.

The buyer suddenly claimed that we had not disclosed that two of our clients were merging and thus would reduce the amount of income earned by the company in the future. This was a complete fabrication. I was in the meetings with the private equity buyer and knew that it was both disclosed and was clearly included in the projections of the business income for the next year. Yet, the buyer claimed they did not know and dropped their offer by $1MM, almost ten percent of the deal.

I advised Henry to move on to the backup buyer, but he decided to accept the offer as is. "Randy, you told me what you thought we could get for this company, and even with the discount, it's still $1 million above that! I'm happy with the result so let's just take the offer."

Even though this story has a happy ending, it's worth noting that buyers sometimes use this tactic at the end of a deal. They call it a "cram down" and it's meant to squeeze the seller down in price. Remember, their goal is to pay as little as possible, so they will be looking for any reason to justify a lower sale price, rational or not.

Cram downs are not the only thing you need to watch out for. You must also make sure that you are continuing to build and grow the business while you are in the sale process. Your company's sale price may even depend on how your business performs during negotiations! Ideally you need to kick into overdrive during the few years before and up through the sales process so that you can finish strong, and get the highest price for your company.

The whole point of running your business full tilt down to the very end of the process is that it ultimately allows you to emotionally and financially say "no" to an overreaching buyer. It is vital that you maintain your walk away power until the sales proceeds hit your bank account. Maintaining your emotional edge can make you millions of extra dollars on the sale.

> " **It is vital that you maintain your walk away power until the sales proceeds hit your bank account.** "

Post-Sale Expectations

Let's imagine that you've made it through closing. You've sold your business. Take a moment to celebrate! Let the accomplishment sick in.

All your hard work has come to fruition, and you can take a moment to breathe. Go on vacation, spend time with your family, and take a break from all the emotional business stress!

The question now is: What are you going to do with your newfound freedom? One of the biggest mistakes we see owners make is they forget to plan for their post-sale life. So much of their identity is wrapped up in being a business owner, that once the sale closes, they seem to lose their reason for getting up every day. If you only focus on your last day in business and never stop to think about what it will be like after a sale, you may be disappointed in the end.

Many owners don't handle this transition well, but you can. You just have to discover what you want and then make your goals explicit. Anything new in life is scary. Selling or transitioning your business is just one more stage in life to which you must adjust. Like everything in the Bulletproof Exit Process, proper preparation is vital.

The world is your oyster! You can start a new company, volunteer, join a board, or take up gardening. Visualize the life you want, then take the steps to get there. Use your time to make a difference in the lives of your family and community. Do the things you never had time to do! Take on new challenges, spend time with your children and your grandchildren, and add value to the world in new ways. The key is to find happiness in every stage of life and fill it with purpose. Make sure you create that kind of life post-exit, so that you can enter it with excitement and newfound gusto.

Action Steps

- Where are you in the business cycle?
- Is your business ready for sale?
- Do you know your competitive advantages?
- Do you know who you will use as an M&A firm?

CHAPTER 11

STEP 7: Thriving After Transition

Jerusalem, Israel 848 B.C–796 B.C.

The days of Solomon brought an unparalleled period of peace and prosperity to ancient Israel. But while Solomon may have enjoyed his days of peace, it was his father who created them. King David was a warrior all the days of his life, and tirelessly fought to turn the nation of Israel from a loosely organized band of independent tribes into a unified kingdom and a regional powerhouse.

David always dreamed of building a temple to the Lord God, but it was not to be in his lifetime. Instead, he amassed natural resources beyond measure so that his son Solomon could carry on his life's work. It took Solomon seven years to build the temple of Jewish worship to their God, Yahweh, and thirteen years to build himself a palace, but by the end of the work, Solomon's constructions surpassed the palaces of any kingdom in the world. The nation of Israel lived in a golden age all the years of Solomon's life because his father, David, was willing to work on a dream that wouldn't see fulfillment until after his death.

Many business owners live for the day they can finally sell their business or transition it to a worthy heir. Unfortunately, many owners don't realize that what happens after the sale may be far more important to their financial and emotional well-being than the actual sale itself. Post-sale is where many owners go awry, which is such a shame because it is the season of life that should be the sweetest.

In fact, many owners suffer from depression or regret after selling their company because they feel like they have lost their identity. If you have spent no time dreaming, determining, or preparing your plans, then you may want to consider postponing your exit until you have a fixed direction for your life post-sale.

> **It requires a different skill set to manage a $30 million-dollar company than it does to manage a $30 million-dollar pool of capital.**

It's also important to keep in mind that when the business sells, it will create a massive liquidity event. It's like winning the lottery! The problem is that it requires a different skill set to manage a $30 million-dollar company than it does to manage a $30 million-dollar pool of capital. *Don't presume that just because you ran a company well you can also run the capital well. They are totally different skills.*

Unfortunately, owners too often lose the money, handle their transition badly, or create feuding among their relatives. After all their hard work, they often end in a place far from the one they envisioned. To avoid this pitfall, take the time to set your goals and expectations for post-sale. It can be the difference between success and failure.

Also, once a sale goes through, think about taking a break from financial decisions for six months to a year so you can clear your head. Develop an Investment Policy Statement so you set parameters on your investing strategy once your break is over. A well thought out Investment Policy Statement should give direction on how much you keep in stocks, bonds, cash, private equity, real estate, crypto-currencies, and more. You should have an experienced and knowledgeable professional help you to create this IPS and implement it in a wise manner. Above all, don't be in a hurry. The biggest mistakes often come from business owners trying to redeploy assets quickly.

Take your time and be wary of those who may want to take advantage of your new wealth or your newfound freedom. Though you will be very proud of yourself for having sold your business for real money, it is best that you keep it private as much as possible.

You should consider asking God to give you direction for your future and that of your family. James 1:5 says: "If any of you lacks wisdom, let him ask God, who gives generously to all without reproach, and it will be given him." This is a period where you need wisdom.

How do you want your post-exit to look? Talk it over with your loved ones, strategize with your trusted advisors, and make a plan. Transitioning from success to significance doesn't happen by itself.

Action Steps

- What is your life going to look like post-sale? What activities are you going to be involved in? Where will you spend your time?
- Do you have trustworthy wealth advisors in place to help you manage your liquidity event and develop a plan to redeploy assets?

CHAPTER 12

It Takes a BraveHeart

Edinburgh, Scotland November 1st, 1292 A.D.

On a dark and stormy night in 1286, a freak accident sealed the fate of an entire kingdom. King Alexander III of Scotland had just gotten married. After a wonderful party celebrating his new bride, he decided to ride off into the dark of night, in the middle of a storm.

Somewhere along the way, the king was separated from his companions by the storm's fury. Alone, his horse lost its footing and plunged over the edge of an embankment. The king was found dead, washed up on the shores of the sea the next morning.

With no surviving heirs, the crown was passed to his granddaughter, Margaret, The Maid of Norway. Unfortunately, the young queen died on her journey to Scotland, so the Guardians of Scotland invited Edward I of England to come up and arbitrate between the competing claims to the throne.

The Guardians invitation to King Edward was a massive mistake. Edward saw the situation as an opportunity to expand his kingdom. Instead of providing arbitration, he demanded that his claim to the feudal overlordship of Scotland be recognized—then invaded Scotland.

With the country in chaos and the aristocracy in full retreat, Edward might have been successful in his bid for Scottish submission—if it had not been for the heroism of William Wallace. After assassinating Sheriff William de Heselrig and making a bold raid on the city of Scone, resistance fighters flocked to Wallace's side. Wallace pressed his advantage, and four months later took his stand at the Battle of Sterling Bridge against a professional English Army of 13,000 trained soldiers.

Though vastly outnumbered, Wallace caught the English by surprise as they were crossing the river over the narrow Sterling Bridge. Waiting for the perfect moment, Wallace sent in a phalanx of spearmen followed by heavy cavalry. The charge broke the English ranks and pushed the retreating army back over the bridge. Under the weight of the fleeing army, the bridge collapsed. The men fortunate enough to escape Wallace's blade met their fate in a watery grave.

After the battle, Wallace took on the mantle of Guardian of Scotland on behalf of John Balliol, the true king of Scotland. Wallace reigned until his defeat at Falkirk and subsequent betrayal and capture by the English. King Edward had Wallace shipped to London to stand trial as a traitor to the crown. When they read his crimes before the court, Wallace had only this to say: "I cannot be a traitor to Edward, for I was never his subject."

William Wallace was sentenced to be tortured and executed, his only crime defending the country he loved so dearly. He was dragged through London, drawn and quartered, and then beheaded. His death ended his life, but not his legacy. Inspired by his courage, Robert the Bruce took up Wallace's mantle, eventually defeating the English and reclaiming the Scottish Crown.

* * * * *

The history of war is the history of man. It has shaped human destiny since the dawn of time, bringing out the worst in people, but also revealing what is best. In the midst of incredibly dark times, solitary torches are born to light the way. Wallace was one of those flames.

The story of William Wallace and those who fought with him inspires me. Not because they were extraordinary fighters or legendary warriors, but because they were the opposite. They were commoners. Wallace's men were peasant farmers and blacksmiths, merchants, and laborers. Most of his men had no horses or titles, no lands or dominions. They didn't fight for gold, or thrones, or kings, or glory. They fought for freedom.

Many of the patriots that fought in the American Revolutionary War descended from these humble Scottish independence fighters. Like their forefathers, the Revolutionaries rose up against the oppression of the British government. They were carpenters and sailors, farmers, and tailors. Paul Revere was a silversmith, George Washington a surveyor and farmer, and John Hancock a merchant. They were no barons of England, they had no titles of nobility, and they fought for no material gain. Instead, our Founding Fathers fought for freedom.

" You must fight for a noble purpose. "

I've used examples from military history throughout this book because they tell a story we need to hear, not because I glory in war. As we saw with Alexander the Great and Richard the Lionheart, it is not enough just to fight well. You must fight for a noble purpose. It makes no difference if you win or lose, if you are fighting for the wrong objective. I have worked with hundreds of business owners over my career, but the ones that stand out are the ones who took action for their families, and for the continuance of their legacies.

The true BraveHearts of the business world accomplish great things for themselves and their families. It's not easy to be successful in this way, but BraveHearts work at it every day. They build a business and run it in such a way that it provides a legacy for generations.

I have loved working with generational families. I have seen that people really do reap what they sow, often in the lives of their children and grandchildren. The parents that ignore their children, coddle them, or neglect to teach them, often end up with broken families. Their children self-destruct and take the business down with them, starting a cycle that sometimes lasts for generations. But the parents that teach their children well in every area of life tend to have families that love each other, work hard, and share common values.

The Golden Rule is golden for a reason. It is the foundation of servant leadership, which is the key hallmark of those who create businesses that last for generations.

One of my favorite examples of such a family is the Williams family. They are a family of hardworking farmers that love their children well. I met them because the first generation asked me to work on their estate planning. At that time the patriarch and matriarch of the family were in their late 80s. They were delightful people, and they both passed away within three years of my work.

We had a seamless transition to their son, but within a few years, the son died as well. Before long, we had made another transition to the three grandsons. But as with many 3rd generation families, we had lost touch, and those in that generation hadn't planned for an untimely exit. The family needed my help with issues related to the death of one of the grandsons who had died leaving a wife and children. We finally resolved the issue, though it took time and there was much heartache.

As with all Braveheart families, they learned a great lesson from that tragic situation. Today, we are working on planning for the fourth generation! They have included the younger generations in every area of their business planning, and understand the importance of generational transition.

It's amazing to see the first generation's values and legacy continue on so many years later. They are truly living the American dream.

The Williams legacy is still alive, in their family and their business. Now, the Williams are not a perfect family. But their dedication to future planning and strong familial relationships has broken the "shirtsleeves to shirtsleeves in three generations" curse. You have the same opportunity!

> ## "It's time for you to write your own roadmap, your own American dream."

You now have the guidebook to enable you to grow a business, build it to be bulletproof, and prepare it for sale or transition. It's time for you to write your own roadmap, your own American dream.

It's time to take this process seriously and actually implement it. Go back through the 7 steps and start to build a *Bulletproof Exit Plan* that creates an enduring legacy.

Start now. It will take time, energy, and investment, but it's the best thing you can do for your family and your business. You can rise up to the challenge and become a true Braveheart.

You can create a legacy of faith, family, and financial security that can last for many generations, but it will take commitment and determination. As you know now, this process isn't for the faint-hearted—it takes one with a Brave Heart!

Now get moving!

Godspeed!

Randy M. Long

EPILOGUE

An Eternal Legacy

"The kingdom of heaven is like a treasure hidden in the field, which a man found and hid again; and from joy over it he goes and sells all that he has and buys that field.

Again, the kingdom of heaven is like a merchant seeking fine pearls, and upon finding one pearl of great price, he went and sold all that he had and bought it."

Jesus of Nazareth

The things we value and treasure the most are things we cannot touch or feel or quantify: love, loyalty, joy, kindness.

To build a lasting legacy is to work for something beyond what we will see, yet more valuable than anything we could ever own.

I have been part of a number of very well-known business-related groups and coaching programs. They encourage us to be the best we can be so we can be wildly successful. We are told to eliminate those around us who get in the way of our goals. It is a very self-focused approach to life, wherein success is measured primarily by how much money you make. Yet I have been in the room when business owners have reached their ultimate financial goals, only to hear them ask, "Is this all there is?" or, to see them begin to sink into depression because what they valued most did not give them joy or peace.

This has driven me back to a verse I learned as a child, that should make us all think about whether we are chasing the wrong treasure. In Matthew 16:26, the Bible says, "For what will it profit a man if he gains the whole world and forfeits his soul? Or what shall a man give in exchange for his soul?" This question is of utmost importance because our souls will live for all eternity. Yet, we cannot earn the right to spend eternity in heaven. Rather God, in his mercy, offers us this gift, through believing in and following Jesus Christ. Ephesians 2:8–9 and many other verses make this point clearly. "For by grace you have been saved through faith. And this is not your own doing; it is the gift of God, not a result of works, so that no one may boast." On the cross, Jesus paid the price for the sins of all who believe in him.

This book partially represents my legacy, my life's work. I have been blessed to know and counsel many entrepreneurs who have had the courage to own their own businesses and sacrifice day in and day out for their families, employees, and clients. It has been a privilege to walk through the trenches with them. I have felt personally connected to each of you and want to end this book with what is closest to my heart.

To all of you Bravehearts, I don't want you to trade what the world offers for what Jesus offers. I do not want you to miss the last best treasure—knowing Jesus as your friend, your Creator, and your Savior. No other person has healed thousands, won every argument against the ruling religious hypocrites, or stopped the wind and the waves with his words. And most incomprehensible of all—giving His life in exchange for us and then miraculously, rising from the dead. What He did not do is almost as astounding as what He did do: He never hurt anyone, He never had an army, He refused an earthly kingdom, He never touched anyone inappropriately, He did not advocate for revolution, He never told a lie or failed to do what He promised. No other political leader, spiritual guide, man, woman, or child even comes close to living this grace filled, perfect life. He had to be the Son of God made flesh, God incarnate.

To my children, friends and family, and you who have happened to pick up this book—I want you to know He has made all the difference in my life. You will not find peace anywhere else. There is no freedom from guilt or true love and acceptance outside of His realm. Yet we cannot work to gain His love and there is nothing we can do to make up for all the wrong in our lives and hearts. That's why Jesus had to die—to receive the judgment of God that we deserve but cannot pay. As He was dying, He said, "tetelestai" translated "it is finished", and there is nothing anyone can add to His ultimate sacrifice. After raising from the dead on the third day, He now stands at God's right hand to help those who trust in Him.

In my blackest night, He was the light. In times when I thought I couldn't go on; He wrapped His arms around me. When I didn't know where to turn, He guided and sustained me. He doesn't want you for his propaganda machine. He doesn't need you to join His army to fight a holy war. He wants you to be adopted as God's child—a child can only bring love and a smile to his father's face.

But you are required to recognize the true value of this incredible gift, in order to receive it. The merchant saw that the pearl was of incomparable value; it was worth giving up everything he had, in order to possess it. The treasure of heaven is costly; the price is the surrender of control of your life. Although what you get in return— to be forgiven, loved, and accepted by the King of the universe—is priceless. My sincere prayer is that you will turn from your sin and answer His call:

"Come, follow me."

CPSIA information can be obtained
at www.ICGtesting.com
Printed in the USA
BVHW032100071022
648870BV00006B/25